'Planned' teenage pregnancy

Perspectives of young parents from disadvantaged backgrounds

Suzanne Cater and Lester Coleman

JOSEPH ROWNTREE
FOUNDATION

First published in Great Britain in June 2006 by

The Policy Press
Fourth Floor, Beacon House
Queen's Road
Bristol BS8 1QU
UK
Tel no +44 (0)117 331 4054
Fax no +44 (0)117 331 4093
Email tpp-info@bristol.ac.uk
www.policypress.org.uk

Published for the Joseph Rowntree Foundation by The Policy Press

ISBN-10 1 86134 837 1
ISBN-13 978 1 86134 837 1

British Library Cataloguing in Publication Data
A catalogue record for this book is available from the British Library.

Library of Congress Cataloging-in-Publication Data
A catalog record for this book has been requested.

Suzanne Cater (Research Officer) and Lester Coleman (Research Team Manager) both work for the Trust for the Study of Adolescence (TSA).

The Trust for the Study of Adolescence (TSA) was founded in 1989 to help improve the lives of young people and families. Our work is derived from the belief that there is a lack of knowledge and understanding about adolescence and young adulthood. The Trust is trying to close this gap through:

- applied research
- training for professionals, and projects that develop professional practice
- publications for parents, professionals and young people
- influencing policy makers, service providers and public opinion.

At present, the majority of our work is focusing on the following areas: health, emotional well-being, parenting and family life, communication, social action and youth justice. New areas of work are also being developed, and TSA is keen to work with other organisations that share our aim of improving the lives of young people.

Trust for the Study of Adolescence
23 New Road, Brighton, East Sussex, UK BN1 1WZ
Tel: 01273 693311, Fax: 01273 679907
Website: www.tsa.uk.com

The **Joseph Rowntree Foundation** has supported this project as part of its programme of research and innovative development projects, which it hopes will be of value to policy makers, practitioners and service users. The facts presented and views expressed in this report are, however, those of the authors and not necessarily those of the Foundation.

Cover design by Qube Design Associates, Bristol
Front cover: photograph supplied by kind permission of www.JohnBirdsall.co.uk
Printed in Great Britain by Hobbs the Printers Ltd, Southampton

This publication can be provided in alternative formats, such as large print, Braille, audiotape and on disk. Please contact: Communications Department, Joseph Rowntree Foundation, The Homestead, 40 Water End, York YO30 6WP. Tel: 01904 615905. Email: info@jrf.org.uk

Introduction

Structure of the report

Background to the research is provided in this first chapter, in which the scale and trends of teenage pregnancy in England are introduced, along with its relationship with poverty and disadvantage. Also introduced are the notions of 'planned' and 'unplanned' pregnancies, and the research that has looked into the evidence for, and explanations behind, planned teenage pregnancy is briefly outlined. The chapter closes by setting this research within the current policy and practice context.

Chapter 2 begins by outlining the main objectives of the research and summarising the main research methods used. It presents some descriptive findings from a brief screening questionnaire that was used to select interviewees, and then outlines the profile and nature of the interview sample.

Chapters 3 to 7 are dedicated to presenting the main findings from the in-depth interviews. Chapter 3 looks at young women's diverse interpretations of planned pregnancy, and also outlines their first reactions to becoming pregnant. Young women's perceptions of how their childhood and background may have affected their decisions to become pregnant are outlined in Chapter 4, while Chapter 5 shows how the need for an alternative lifecourse and positive preferences for parenthood affected this decision. Pre- and post-parenthood experiences are illustrated in Chapter 6, with particular emphasis on young women's reflections on their decisions and future expectations. Two contrasting case studies are also included. Chapter 7 presents themes derived exclusively from young fathers, concentrating on the similarities and differences compared with earlier findings.

Conclusions and a focus on the implications for policy and practice are provided in Chapter 8.

Background to the research

The reduction of teenage conception rates has been prioritised by the government, with the Teenage Pregnancy Unit (established in 1999) leading on this 10-year strategy. In 2003, for every 1,000 young women aged 15-17 in England, 42 became pregnant. This latest available rate equates to a 9.8% decline since 1998 (ONS, 2005). Although this progress is encouraging, it will clearly be a tough challenge to meet the Teenage Pregnancy Strategy's target of halving the under-18 conception rate between 1999 and 2010. Although it is not possible to compare conception rates across Europe, it is reported that the rates of teenage *births* (in other words, conceptions that resulted in live births) in the UK are the highest in Western Europe: around five times those in the Netherlands, three times those in France and twice those in Germany (UNICEF, 2001). With the cost to the National Health Service of pregnancy among under-18s estimated at over £63 million a year (Dennison, 2004), some argue that it is understandable that the reduction of teenage pregnancy has been afforded such priority.

There is marked variation throughout England in teenage conception rates. Fifty per cent of under-18 conceptions occur in the 20% of census wards with the highest rates (SEU, 1999). These variations have been linked to specific population groups, such as looked-after children and care leavers (Biehal et al, 1992), young offenders (Hobcraft, 1998), and children of teenage mothers (Kiernan, 1995; Ermisch and Pevalin, 2003). There is also strong and growing evidence linking teenage pregnancy to poor school attendance and low educational attainment (Wellings et al, 2001).

In addition to the above, much has been documented about the strong association between teenage pregnancy and poverty and disadvantage. Research using the ONS Longitudinal Study (Botting et al, 1998) has shown that the risk of becoming a teenage mother is almost 10 times higher for a girl whose family is in social class V (unskilled manual), than for those in social class I (professional). Living in local authority housing (as opposed to owner-occupied) is associated with a three-fold increase in the likelihood of a teenage girl becoming pregnant. This strong and unequivocal association has formed the basis for focusing this research on young people from more poor and disadvantaged backgrounds. In view of the negative outcomes associated with teenage pregnancy, youthful parenthood has been viewed both as a consequence *and* a cause of poverty and disadvantage. In reviewing recent research evidence, Dennison (2004) writes:

> ... those who had been teenage
> mothers had experienced more socio-
> economic deprivation, more mental
> health difficulties and drug problems,
> had lower levels of educational
> attainment, and were more likely to be
> living in deprived neighbourhoods.
> (Dennison, 2004, p 7)

Of interest, Ermisch and Pevalin (2003) report findings from a longitudinal study looking at the outcomes of young women who became parents as teenagers, while controlling for social class. They found that these women were more likely to partner men who were poorly qualified and unemployed, relative to those women who were not teenage parents. Ermisch and Pevalin report that this tends to have the subsequent effect of reducing the standard of living for the woman and her children, thus acting as a further cause of poverty and disadvantage. Aside to faring worse in the 'marriage market', this influential study is particularly interesting in that it

provides an alternative stance towards teenage pregnancy. The study concludes that a 'teen birth has little impact on a woman's qualifications, employment or earnings when they are 30 years of age' (Ermisch and Pevalin, 2003, p 3). This argument can be extended to support the notion that teenage parents from poor and disadvantaged areas are, in fact, no worse off than similar aged young people from such areas. Rather than teenage parenthood per se influencing their outcomes, it is apparent that a background of poverty and disadvantage is of greater significance. In this manner, the Ermisch and Pevalin (2003) study differs from the government's primarily negative social construction of teenage pregnancy and its apparent preventive focus on reducing conception rates (Phoenix, 1993). By contrast, it asserts that young people can make positive decisions to become parents, with minimal ill-effects over the longer term. Positive decisions for teenage parenthood, as will be revealed, is a core theme evident throughout this research report.

However, Ermisch and Pevalin's (2003) findings have also been contested by other research, which has shown that teenage motherhood does have adverse consequences above and beyond the cohort effects associated with deprivation. For example, longitudinal research published by the Department for Education and Skills (DfES, 2005a) shows that teenage pregnancy is an important mediating factor for exacerbating the poorer consequences associated with material deprivation. The inconclusive evidence is further illustrated by the poorer mental health reported by teenage mothers two years after birth (Ermisch and Pevalin, 2003).

Although there is a large amount of quantitative, macro-level evidence supporting the relationship between teenage pregnancy and poverty and disadvantage, less is known about *how* this relationship exists, or the decisions that may take place. Indeed, most of the research into teenagers' decision making has concerned the option of terminating the pregnancy. Tabberer et al (2000) explored teenagers' decisions regarding an unplanned pregnancy. It was found that decisions to terminate the pregnancy were shaped by a range of factors, including the prevalence and visibility of teenage motherhood within the local area. Another important factor was the community-wide view on terminating a pregnancy. Lee et al (2004) found that teenagers in some affluent parts of the country are four times more likely to terminate a pregnancy than those in some more deprived areas. It was found that teenagers' personal situations, rather than their moral views, were the biggest influence on the decision. Those who were facing poverty and disadvantage were generally more 'pro-life' due to deeply embedded factors entwined in social deprivation, the attitudes of family and friends and the accepted behavioural norms in their communities (where youthful pregnancy is more common). Moreover, those who perceived their lives as insecure and unsettled were more likely to see becoming a parent as a positive change. By contrast, those who had plans to go on to further education and a career were more likely to choose a termination. A newspaper headline on the day this research was revealed read: 'Pregnant teenagers live in different worlds: the rich have abortions, the poor have babies' (*The Times*, 30 June 2004). These conclusions are supported by Turner (2004), who also found that young women from deprived backgrounds were more likely to predict that they would keep a baby. The author explains this is terms of an 'acceptance' theory. That is, having low expectations (arguably more prominent in poor and disadvantaged areas) can cause young people to be more accepting of what happens *to* them, including pregnancy.

Aside to the termination or continuation of pregnancy, less research has attempted to explore the decision-making processes *prior* to conception (McAllister and Clarke, 1998; Swann et al, 2003). Although it is commonly assumed that the vast majority of teenage pregnancies are unplanned or accidental, it may be the case that planning underlies a proportion of these pregnancies. The research presented in this report serves to bridge this gap in the evidence base, by exploring the decisions behind planned teenage pregnancy among those facing poverty and disadvantage.

Entwined with researching this decision making is the challenge of distinguishing between planned and unplanned pregnancies. In researching this area, it must be recognised that these are terms that are rarely used by teenagers in relation to their pregnancy (Finlay, 1996). Indeed, Fischer et al (1999) conducted a qualitative study to explore how women relate to the variety of terms used to define the intention status of pregnancies. It was found that definitions of terms varied substantially among women, and seemed to be correlated to social and cultural influences. The concepts of 'wanted' and 'unwanted' pregnancies were qualitatively distinct from the concepts of 'planned' and 'unplanned' pregnancies and seemed to be more relevant to decision making regarding the possibility of a termination of pregnancy. Furthermore, in the qualitative stage of a study aiming to develop a new measure of pregnancy planning/intention (see p 9), Barrett and Wellings (2002) found that women tend not to use the terms spontaneously when discussing the circumstances of their pregnancy. Women were able to explain the terms, but there was notable variation in their understanding. Women tended to only apply the term 'planned' if four criteria were met in their previous accounts during the interview. These were intending to become pregnant, stopping contraception, partner agreement and reaching the right time in terms of lifestyle/life stage. 'Unplanned' was a term used to cover a variety of circumstances. In the same study, Barrett and Wellings also highlighted the fact that although large national surveys have measured planning/intention status using multidimensional questions, there is a lack of validity and need for some consistency in this research (echoed by Swann et al, 2003). In light of this argument, this report provides a brief outline of how young women interviewed in this study defined planning in the context of pregnancy (Chapter 3).

In response to the need for a more consistent approach to measurement, Barrett et al (2004) devised a valid and reliable measure of planned/unplanned pregnancy: the London Measure of Unplanned Pregnancy or LMUP questionnaire. The measure is thought to be appropriate for today's modern demographic trends (for example, people in different types of relationships), and was found to be highly acceptable to women in terms of language and time taken to complete. The measure is a six-item, tick-box questionnaire, and is suitable for use with any pregnant woman regardless of outcome and age. The development of this measure involved 67 interviews with pregnant (continuing with pregnancy and having a termination) and recently pregnant (post-termination and postnatal) women from eight different health service providers in different areas of the UK. Psychometric testing among 1,041 women (including 104 women under 20) showed that the measure is highly reliable (Cronbach's a=0.92; test-retest reliability=0.97). The LMUP was also found to have high face, content and construct validity. This means that the LMUP measures what it proclaims to measure, in terms of the whole questionnaire and individual questions. The advantages of this measure are that it does not make any assumptions about the nature of women's relationships, it does not assume that women have fully-formed childbearing plans, it does not assume any sort of family building, and it is suitable for any pregnancy regardless of outcome. The fact that a woman can score between 0 and 12 means that women are not categorised dichotomously (that is, only planned or unplanned), but can have a range of positions regarding pregnancy planning. This is a more realistic way of looking at fertility decisions, as behaviour is not always in line with intentions, and some women are clearly more ambivalent than others. Given its credibility, this questionnaire was used in our study to identify those who viewed their pregnancy more as planned.

Aside to addressing the complex definitions of planned pregnancies, it is equally important to draw reference to previous studies that have researched this area, both in terms of the *prevalence* of planned pregnancies, and the *explanations* behind such pregnancies. Although there has been little overall research in this area, evidence of planned pregnancies is available in the LMUP validation study (Barrett et al, 2004) and in the tracking survey carried out as part of the evaluation of the government's Teenage Pregnancy Strategy. In the first year of the latter, 106 women reported becoming pregnant before the age of 18. Of these, 10% had scores of 10-12 on the LMUP (that is, high degree of planning), 43% had scores of 4-9, and 47% had scores of 0-3 (that is, low degree of planning) (BMRB, 2001). Data from the second year show that of 96 women who reported becoming pregnant before 18, 3% had scores of 10-12, 32% had scores of 4-9, and 65% had scores of 0-3 (BMRB, 2003). In

addition, Kiernan (1995) and MacDonald and Marsh (2005) also identified evidence of planned teenage pregnancy in their studies, this time specifically among those from poor and disadvantaged backgrounds.

The current policy focus on unplanned teenage pregnancy suggests that teenagers only become pregnant due to failed contraception, and/or a lack of knowledge, and/or poor contraception negotiation skills (see policy and practice context of the research, pp 5-7). Although the Social Exclusion Unit (SEU, 1999) report acknowledges that planned pregnancy in teenagers exists, the policy focus is very much on unplanned pregnancy. This is mainly due to the lack of information regarding how common planned pregnancy is in young people. The growing evidence to suggest that some teenagers' pregnancies have elements of planning challenges the stereotypical viewpoint that teenage parents are a homogeneous group (JRF, 1999). This view is also evident in the Teenage Pregnancy Strategy, which outlines that, 'in practice, the first conscious decision that many teenagers make about their pregnancy is whether to have an abortion or to continue with the pregnancy' (SEU, 1999, p 28). In reality, parenthood is a preferred option for some teenagers. The policy emphasis is skewed more towards the prevention of unplanned pregnancies, which lends support to the claims that the UK has an overwhelmingly negative social construction of teenage motherhood (Phoenix, 1993). In a way, young mothers are frequently viewed as both an 'at risk' group within society and a 'risk to' society (Mitchell and Green, 2002). Research into this area will challenge such stereotypes, and support the work of those who ask 'why should some young women *not* become pregnant and have children?' (Arai, 2003). Indeed, Arai (2003) suggests that having children young could be a sign of maturity, as opposed to immaturity, because many young mothers have experienced significant adversity and view parenthood as a meaningful option. Furthermore, society's negative view of teenage pregnancy was once again illustrated by recently released research by the YWCA (2005). This highlighted the prevalence of the stereotypical viewpoint that young women get pregnant to get a local authority house and, consequently, the YWCA continues to challenge the Teenage Pregnancy Strategy to put more emphasis on supporting teenage mothers, as well as working in a preventive way. The research reported here will go some way to further challenge these stereotypical views.

Although there is growing evidence of planned teenage pregnancy, little research has explored the reasons behind this. Murray (1990) was one of the first to formally put forward the idea that teenage pregnancies are planned in order to gain access to local authority housing and welfare. Murray, an American social policy expert who influenced debate in the US and the UK, has controversial opinions about single parents, and saw the majority of teenage pregnancies as planned. Although there appears to be a commonly held, near-mythical belief in the right-wing press that young women intentionally become pregnant to gain access to local authority housing, there exists research to the contrary that suggests that young women are not actually aware of what they are entitled to from the system until they become pregnant (Allen and Bourke-Dowling, 1998), and are also more likely to be living with their parents (YWCA, 2005). In contrast with Murray's (1990) work, the limited research in this area draws most explanation for teenage pregnancies from the links between poverty and disadvantage and low expectations (SEU, 1999; Arai, 2003; Turner, 2004). With low expectations and a perceived lack of life options, young people from more deprived areas seemingly have less incentive to avoid pregnancy (although arguably distinct from a planned pregnancy), and hold a more fatalistic view towards 'falling pregnant', as opposed to seeing it as an outcome they have a choice about.

A particularly notable study by Montgomery (2001, 2002), in the US, was one of the few to explore thoroughly the motivations behind planned adolescent pregnancy. The author found that themes could be divided into two broad categories. One category explains the planning of the pregnancy, while the other relates to the actual pregnancy. Themes related to planning the pregnancy were further divided into 'needs' and 'wants'. 'Needs' included important criteria that were necessary for pregnancy, including: financial, relationship and age-related goals; the boyfriend's involvement in planning (at least to some

extent); environmental issues; and the need for stability. 'Wants' included: the desire to be perceived as more grown up, with increased responsibility, independence and maturity; a long history of desiring pregnancy and the maternal role; never having had anything to call their own, and wanting someone to care for and love; and feeling that pregnancy was the natural step in their life or relationship with their boyfriend. Although this study was only based on eight young women who planned their pregnancies, the multifactorial themes generated are of great interest and relevance to this study reported here. Most of the reasons were attached to adulthood, and a sense of control over their future, and the authors suggest that 'these adolescents are telling us through their pregnancies that they need to be respected and helped to grow into productive citizens' (Mongomery, 2001, p 27).

Policy and practice context of the research

As mentioned earlier (p 4), the policy context surrounding teenage pregnancy is focused on supporting parents and the prevention of unplanned pregnancies, with less recognition of young people choosing to become parents. This minimal recognition is hampered by a lack of knowledge in the area of planned teenage pregnancy.

By focusing more on the prevention of unplanned pregnancies, the government's Teenage Pregnancy Strategy (SEU, 1999) has been criticised for not providing more support for young parents (YWCA, 2005). Other recent policy initiatives include the landmark Green Paper *Every child matters* (DfES, 2003), which aims to reduce the number of children who become teenage parents. In addition, the recent Public Health White Paper, *Choosing health: Making healthy choices easier* (DH, 2004), includes an investment of £300 million to help achieve its goals over the next three years. Again, there is little acknowledgement towards young people who plan to become pregnant. However, the White Paper sets very sensible and important policy objectives for young people. It aims to ensure that young people 'understand the real risks of unprotected sex and to persuade them of the benefits of using condoms to avoid the risk of sexually transmitted infections or unplanned pregnancies' (DH, 2004, p 5). *Youth matters*, the recent Green Paper (DfES, 2005b), further highlights the growing recognition of young people's health needs.

In terms of current practice, the emphasis towards unplanned pregnancies is again evident. As a guide to 'what works' in preventing pregnancy, the Swann et al (2003) review of reviews highlights school-based sex and relationships education, community-based education, youth development programmes and family outreach. Additionally, in a recent controversial step, Beverly Hughes (Minister for Children, Young People and Families) told *The Guardian* that government had reached the limits of its ability to reduce the UK's teenage pregnancy rate and now parents needed to 'take the initiative' and start talking to their children about sex. She added that they would be supported by Sure Start and government-funded helplines (*The Guardian*, 26 May 2005, p 12).

The primary focus on unplanned pregnancies has lead some researchers to suggest that the government has a rather limited view of young motherhood. The policies, according to Arai (2003), lack imagination and focus on improved access to contraception and better sex education. While this is necessary, current policies do not tackle the fact that intentions, planning and decision making around pregnancy are complex. It could be that most women, even very young women, *do* actually make decisions about when they have children. Current policy fails to recognise that some young women will become pregnant because they feel it is the right decision for them, regardless of the services available and guidance offered (Geronimus, 1997).

It is clear that further research is needed to gain more insight into the mechanisms that lead young people to choose early pregnancy and parenthood, and also the reasons why they are *not* taking the preventive advice and information offered to them in sex and relationships education and innovative interventions in schools (for example, 'Baby think it over' simulators [Somers and Fahlman, 2001]). Such research would help professionals to work confidently and effectively with young

people to help them to consider life-choices other than young parenthood. Where this life-choice is made, professionals should be well-equipped with the appropriate knowledge and expertise so that services ensure the best care for both parents and babies, in terms of ongoing support regarding education and appropriate housing according to age and needs. Greene (2003) argues that current policy fails to reflect the complexities surrounding teenage pregnancy and could exacerbate, rather than alleviate, young mothers' experiences of social exclusion. Corlyon and McGuire (1999) suggest that professionals working with vulnerable young people who are experiencing poverty and disadvantage should remember that they are not accustomed to feeling in control, and so are not familiar with long-term planning. They are, therefore, a high-risk group for teenage pregnancy.

This research argues that there exists a need for new materials/resources for professionals in order that they can work effectively with young people who have planned their pregnancy. Such materials would serve to voice the young people's views and opinions, and help professionals to realise their individual needs. This is important, because their situations and needs are likely to be different from those of young people reporting unplanned pregnancies. It is intended that materials will be developed from this research, in order that the issue of planned teenage pregnancy can be highlighted in work with young people.

In summary, this review of the closely related literature has highlighted some significant gaps in the evidence base. Primarily, little research has explored teenagers' decisions *prior* to conception, and the notion that some teenagers plan their pregnancies. The emphasis has been on the avoidance of unplanned pregnancies among teenagers, and subsequent decisions around the continuation or termination of pregnancy. The limited research suggests, however, that low expectations and thus a desire *not* to avoid pregnancy, appears to play a role. Young men's views have been totally excluded from research. There is a lack of research into the extent of, and explanations for, planned teenage pregnancy. This confusion means there is the risk that the support needs of those who planned or are planning to become young parents may be overlooked. It could be that pregnancies in young women are frequently assumed to be accidental, and it is also possible that young women who planned to become pregnant do not always correct this assumption. Reasons for this could be due to the social stigma of getting pregnant 'on purpose', and the associated connotations. A deeper insight will be of value to practitioners working with young people and young parents (in recognising the motivations for pregnancy and identifying specific support needs), and policy makers who lay the emphasis primarily on unplanned pregnancies.

2

Objectives, methods and introductory findings from the research

Introduction

In this chapter the main research objectives and research methods will be outlined. Two sets of introductory findings will then be presented. First, findings from screening questionnaires that were used to select a sample of interviewees. Second, some findings from the female interviewees in terms of their socio-demographic profile and other commonly shared characteristics.

Research objectives and methods

In providing an exploration into planned teenage pregnancy, the research has identified the following two key objectives:

- To explore the decisions behind 'planned' teenage pregnancy among those facing poverty and disadvantage.
- To assess the policy implications of the findings.

It is important to stress at the outset that this research will only include the views and experiences of young people who are facing poverty and disadvantage. There are a number of reasons for this sample emphasis. As we have seen in Chapter 1, teenage pregnancy rates are higher in areas with lower socioeconomic status. Tentative evidence suggests that those in more deprived areas are more likely to choose this life option (Murray, 1990; SEU, 1999; Arai, 2003; Turner, 2004). It is hoped that the views of such a sample will help to show *why* young people in these areas are more prone to teenage pregnancy and choosing to become a young parent. It was not possible to include a comparison group of young people from less deprived areas who also planned their pregnancies; however, without this comparison group, this research is unable to definitively answer how poverty and disadvantage, *as opposed to other factors*, influence teenagers' decisions to plan their pregnancies.

In an area of such little previous research, it is particularly appropriate to use qualitative methods that allow explanations and findings, perhaps as yet unanticipated or unknown, to arise inductively from the data. Indeed, a qualitative exploration into this area was recommended in the extensive review into teenage pregnancy initiatives undertaken by Swann et al (2003). In order to meet the objectives of the research, it was considered appropriate to use semi-structured, in-depth interviews. In total, 51 interviews were completed (41 with young mums or mums-to-be, and 10 with young fathers).

Young people were selected purposively (that is, non-randomly) for the interviews. The sample was all White British. Young people were selected according to the following criteria:

- reported a pregnancy that was planned (see p 9 for a precise definition);
- either pregnant or already a parent of a child less than one year old;
- aged 19 or under prior to the planned pregnancy;
- currently experiencing (or experienced in the past) relatively high levels of poverty and disadvantage;
- varying geographical location and rural/ urban classification;

- volunteered for interview and gave their contact details.

The remaining part of this chapter and Chapters 3 to 6 inclusive will deal exclusively with the 41 young mums and mums-to-be who were interviewed. Chapter 7 will present the findings from the 10 young fathers alongside the associated research methods, which were slightly different.

As noted in Chapter 1, the London Measure of Unplanned Pregnancy (LMUP) questionnaire (devised and validated by Barrett et al, 2004) was integral in ensuring that we only interviewed those who planned their pregnancy. This screening questionnaire, attached in full as Appendix A, consisted of items asking about the following:

Q1: Contraception use
Q2: Timing of being pregnant
Q3: Intentions regarding pregnancy (just before they became pregnant)
Q4: Whether they wanted a baby (just before they became pregnant)
Q5: Whether they improved their health just before pregnancy (for example, by taking folic acid)
Q6: The extent to which they had discussed pregnancy matters with their partner (just before they became pregnant)

The multiple choice answers were scored according to how they related to planning (for example, in Question 1, (two) maximum points were awarded for 'I/we were not using any contraception'). The majority of the young people who were interviewed scored between eight and 12 (with 12 being the maximum possible score for planning). Although this questionnaire was used in identifying the majority of the female interviewees, a small proportion (six out of the 41) were approached based on the recommendation of a project worker. The project worker identified the women, as they knew their pregnancies were planned, and hence the questionnaires were not necessary in these instances.

Meeting the remaining eligibility criteria, in particular the geographical spread, was achieved by careful selection of the recruitment sites. These sites were typically young mums' groups or support groups located in different parts of England. The latter were mainly young parent groups at Sure Start centres, or groups led by health visitors and/or midwives. After initial contact with the project worker, batches of the LMUP questionnaire were sent out and returned by Freepost to the Trust for the Study of Adolescence (TSA). Typically, once four to six eligible young people were identified, the researcher then visited the site in person to undertake the interviews. To ensure a varied sample, this purposive sampling became more focused throughout the fieldwork, for example, contacting groups from relatively more rural areas to guarantee their inclusion in the sample. TSA contacts proved particularly useful in identifying suitable sites for questionnaire administration (for example, a Young Father's project and recruitment recommendations from the National Teenage Parent Research and Practice Group). Postcode data from the questionnaires were used to indicate levels of poverty and disadvantage (see pp 13-14).

Fellow researchers at TSA and members of our Project Advisory Group helped refine the interview schedule, which was eventually piloted among four young mums in East Sussex. The interview schedule opens very informally by exploring the young people's first experiences of pregnancy (for example, how old they were, how they found out, who they told, the father's reaction, and so on). To confirm information retrieved through the LMUP questionnaire, the interview then explores the extent to which this pregnancy was planned. The main body of the interview asks specifically how childhood and family history, income, housing, and place of residence (including locality) may have influenced their decision making regarding pregnancy. These questions are separated into 'when growing up as a child' and also 'in the year prior to pregnancy'. The influence of educational achievement, future ambitions, and employment/training experiences and aspirations are then discussed, alongside the influences of family, friends and sexual partners. Crucially, through its inductive approach, the interview permits other explanations behind this decision making to arise that are not possible to anticipate in advance. The interview closes by asking participants to reflect on their life prior to pregnancy (and how different their life may be now), and also imagine their life in the future.

This unearthed some of the leading expectations and outcomes of pregnancy and also identified the types of support young people said they needed most. On average, the interview took about 45 minutes to complete and was tape-recorded (where consent was given). Appropriate ethical considerations were adopted in conducting the research. Consent was obtained prior to interview, the participants were aware of the right to not answer questions or to terminate the interview at any time, confidentiality was stressed, and detail was provided on how the research findings would be used. At the end of the interview, feedback from the study's findings at a later date was offered, and a £10 voucher was issued to cover time and any travel expenses. Throughout the research process, the ethics guidelines published by TSA were followed[1].

All quantitative data from the screening questionnaire were coded, entered and analysed in SPSS (Statistical Package for the Social Sciences). All tape-recorded data from the interviews were transcribed verbatim, coded and entered into QSR N6/NuDist (qualitative data analysis software). There were three distinct stages to the analysis of the qualitative data. First, a thematic analysis was performed across the entire sample to explore teenagers' reports and explanations for their planned pregnancy (Chapters 3 to 5). This analysis focused on the generation of common themes and explanations derived from the transcripts. A set of 'master themes' derived from the first few transcripts were compared with those generated through the remaining transcripts. Recurring themes that emerged through this process reflected the shared views and perceptions among participants of the phenomena under investigation. Second, a number of more detailed case studies were performed, to link people's own childhoods and background history to the time approaching pregnancy and birth, through to the present day where reflections and future expectations were also noted (Chapter 6). Third, a separate analysis was performed

among the young dads in our sample, to compare and determine any differences by gender (Chapter 7). To increase the validity of the thematic interpretation, a number of different researchers at TSA coded and analysed the first five transcripts, and agreed a suitable coding frame to guide the ongoing qualitative analysis. The report now turns to the presentation of some introductory research findings.

Findings from the LMUP screening questionnaire

As noted earlier, the LMUP questionnaire was used in order to ensure that eligibility criteria were fulfilled. Crucially, using this questionnaire ensured that only young people who had planned their pregnancy were interviewed. It should be recognised at the outset that the sample completing these questionnaires was selected opportunistically, and is not statistically representative of all young women, parents or parents-to-be. Although the results should be treated with some degree of caution, they do provide an interesting introduction to young people's perceptions of how planned their pregnancy was. Moreover, these findings were particularly informative in shaping the early drafts of the interview schedule.

In total, 29 sites assisted in distributing questionnaires to the young mums or mums-to-be in their group(s). This was negotiated via telephone conversations, e-mails and letters, during which the research was thoroughly explained. The number of questionnaires sent ranged between 10 and 40, depending on the number of groups running, and the size of these groups. In total, 600 questionnaires were sent out to project workers for distribution to young women, of which 185 were actually distributed. The remaining questionnaires, some 400 or so, were never distributed by the project workers. This is likely to reflect the work pressures faced at the various sites, combined with reports that fewer than expected numbers of young parents, or parents-to-be, attended the groups. Feedback from the project workers in the 29 sites informed us that only six young people preferred not to complete the questionnaire,

---

[1] This is a regularly updated document and provides information on protecting participants in research, informed consent, confidentiality and the use of information, feedback, disclosure, expenses, payment and organisational matters.

resulting in 179 being returned (yielding a response rate of 97%).

Findings from all 179 young women completing the LMUP questionnaire:

The wide geographical distribution of those 179 women completing the LMUP questionnaires is shown in Figure 1.

Figure 1: Location of young women completing the LMUP questionnaires

Source: Geospec, University of Brighton

Women completing the questionnaires ranged from 14 to 25 years old (mean age of 18.37 years). The majority of those completing the questionnaires, or 63%, were between the ages of 16 and 19 inclusive. A profile of the scores derived from this questionnaire, ranging from 0 to 12 (with 12 being the maximum possible score of reported planning), is reported in Table 1.

Table 1: Scores derived from the LMUP (total sample)

LMUP score	Number of interviewees	%
0-2 (low degree of 'planning')	31	17.3
3-5	72	40.2
6-8	38	21.3
9-12 (high degree of 'planning')	38	21.1
Total	179	100[a]
Mean score = 5.6		

Note: [a] Percentages are rounded up/down, so occasionally do not equal 100%.

Findings from the sub-sample of 35 interviewees completing the LMUP questionnaire:

Of the 41 interviewees, 35 young women completed a questionnaire. Most of the interviewees (72%) scored between 8 and 12. However, as the selection process progressed, we chose to interview a few young people who scored lower, based largely on their response to what we considered to be one of the most important questions. After using the questionnaire for some time in this research, we chose to assume that if a person reported that 'just before I became pregnant I intended to get pregnant' (Question 3), they were considered as eligible to interview. A detailed breakdown of the interviewee scores from the 35 who completed the questionnaires, presenting a mean score of 9.4 (compared with 5.6 for the total sample completing the questionnaires), is outlined in Figure 2.

It was also apparent that the above scores showed a distinct pattern with age at pregnancy, with the older teenagers reporting a greater degree of planning (Table 2). This may reflect that older age groups are more likely to plan their pregnancies, but also perhaps the younger age groups are more reluctant to admit that they had planned their pregnancy. In the interviews with the youngest women we found some evidence to support the latter.

Figure 2: LMUP questionnaire scores of interviewees

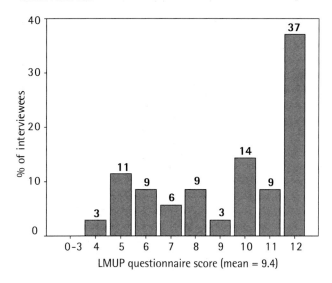

Figure 3: Age range of young women at first 'planned' pregnancy

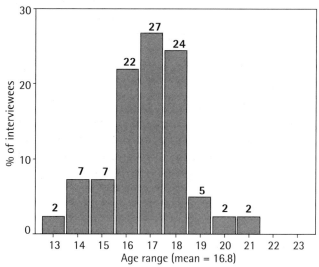

Table 2: Scores derived from the LMUP (interviewees only)

Age at 'planned' pregnancy	Mean score on questionnaire	Number of interviewees (%)	
14	8.0	3	(8.6)
15	5.3	3	(8.6)
16	10.3	7	(20)
17	9.2	9	(25.7)
18	9.6	9	(25.7)
19	12.0	2	(5.6)
20	12.0	1	(2.9)
21	11.0	1	(2.9)
Total	9.4	35	(100)

Figure 4: Age range of young women at interview

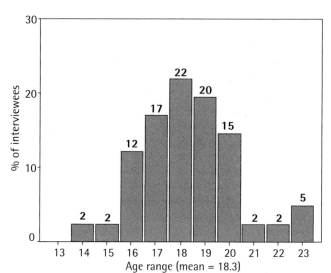

Profile of all 41 interviewees

This section will present findings concerning the socio-demographic profile of all 41 female interviewees.

Age

Of the 41 young women interviewed, two measures of age were recorded: age at becoming pregnant at their first planned pregnancy (Figure 3), and age at interview (Figure 4). For the former, all except two of the women were aged 19 or under, in line with our eligibility criteria.

The discrepancy in age profiles reflects the fact that, in a few cases, some time had passed between pregnancy and interview. It should be noted that, when reporting quotations throughout this report, age at first planned conception is presented.

Parental status

Of the interviewees, the vast majority (34, or 83%) were now parents, with the remaining seven (17%) pregnant with their first planned pregnancy. Also, of those 34 who were parents at interview, 10 had more than one child, of which eight were planned. For these interviewees, the experience of having their first planned pregnancy (the focus of the interview) had not deterred them from planning pregnancies in the future.

It should be noted that approximately 29 of the 41 young women interviewed were still together with the father of their child, although obviously some relationships were more secure than others. The remaining 12 young women had split up from their partner and were single or seeing a new partner. This is interesting because stereotypes dictate that teenage mothers tend to be single and not with the father of their child, but this was not common in this study.

Geographical spread and urban/rural classification

The female interviewees in this study were recruited from a range of geographical locations as shown in Figure 5. These locations varied by region and rural/urban classification, with the more rural locations principally in the South West. The distinction between rural and urban areas was based on whether the majority of the population falls inside a settlement of 10,000 or more (as classified by the Office for National Statistics).

Teenage pregnancy rates, by ward

In further illustration of the interviewee profile, it is interesting to observe the under-18 pregnancy rates (rate per 1,000 women aged 15 to 17) from the census wards where they were located (derived from their postcodes). As outlined in Table 3, the recruitment areas contributed a higher mean rate higher than the national rate (ONS, 2005).

Figure 5: Location of young women interviewees

Source: Geospec, University of Brighton

Poverty and disadvantage

All interviewees were experiencing a significant level of poverty and disadvantage, in accordance with the recruitment sites from which they were selected. The extent of this poverty and disadvantage was assessed in two main ways. First, based on a person's postcode, all interviewees were matched to one of 32,482 Super Output Areas (SOAs) across England. These SOAs, based on an average population of approximately 1,500, are ranked according to an Index of Multiple Deprivation, with 1 being the most deprived, and 32,482 the least deprived. The Index of Multiple Deprivation is a summary measure, incorporating seven domains relating to: income deprivation; employment deprivation; health deprivation and disability; education, skills and training deprivation; barriers to

Table 3: Ward teenage pregnancy rates (interviewees)

Female interviewees (*n*=41)			National rate (England)
Lowest teenage pregnancy rate/ward	Highest teenage pregnancy rate/ward	Mean teenage pregnancy rate of sample wards	
19.5 / Crawley Down and Turner's Hill (South East)	120.2 / Central Worthing (South East)	53.9	42.1

housing and services; living environment deprivation; and crime. While the Index of Multiple Deprivation may be partially limited in its power to describe the individual experience of poverty and disadvantage, it enables a comparison of poverty and disadvantage relative to other areas. As can be shown in Table 4, all the interviewees lived in areas that were experiencing high levels of poverty and disadvantage relative to other areas in the country (69.7% were from the upper quartile of SOAs according to their Index of Multiple Deprivation).

A second insight into young people's experiences of poverty and disadvantage was derived from the experiences revealed from the in-depth interviews. These interviews explored experiences of poverty and disadvantage during early life, as well as in the year immediately prior to becoming pregnant. From this exploration, greater insights into poverty and disadvantage were evident, and were classified into *materialistic* and *emotional* elements. Of these, all the young people in the sample experienced the following in the lists below to a significant extent, either during their own childhood or in the year prior to their pregnancy (obviously, these two time classifications are not mutually exclusive). Background factors and more recent experiences often overlapped, especially for younger interviewees:

Material disadvantage during childhood:

- Parents separated/divorced
- Parents unemployed or in manual jobs
- Moved areas frequently
- 'Disliked' area/location
- Local authority accommodation
- Numerous siblings (overcrowded accommodation)
- Family claiming benefits

- Money 'a worry'
- Poor health and health of immediate family
- Evidence of alcohol and/or drugs misuse within the family

Material disadvantage in the year prior to pregnancy:
- Unsettled living arrangements (for example, thrown out of home, living in temporary accommodation)
- Dissatisfaction with education
- Lack of money due to unemployment, working in a manual job, or at school or college (but wanting to leave)

In addition, and in terms of emotional disadvantage (obviously harder to measure) the majority had experienced the following to a significant extent:

- Negative relationships in the immediate family (that is, violent and volatile)
- Bullying at school
- Lack of open communication, and feeling unable to tell anyone in the family about personal issues
- Lack of encouragement (for example, regarding education, ambitions and general life direction)
- Separation from their partner with whom they became pregnant intentionally

By way of further illustration, a young woman who became pregnant at age 15 describes her background. Her experiences are typical of the young women interviewed in this study. As will be shown in forthcoming chapters, this evident disadvantage was integral in shaping motivations towards pregnancy and teenage parenthood:

Table 4: Index of Multiple Deprivation (interviewees)

Super Output Area rank based on Index of Multiple Deprivation	England (%)	Study sample of interviewees (%)
1 to 8,121	25	69.7
8,122 to 16,242	25	24.3
16,243 to 24,363	25	3
24,364 to 32,482	25	3
Total	100	100

'Like, at that time, I wasn't bothered
about it – well, I was – if it [pregnancy]
happened I would be happy anyway –
it didn't matter if I really messed up
and that – 'cos I mean, I never bonded
with my mum, 'cos like, I never lived
with my mum properly – because (um)
I hadn't never lived with her at a young
age [in care]. I think she don't
understand ... she wasn't there to talk
to me about the Pill and all that kind of
thing ... I had a really bad childhood –
(um) how can I explain it? It's the worst
thing ever. But it made me stronger in
who I am. I lived with my grandma for
a bit, and then my grandma died –
when my grandma died – (um) things
was getting for the worst – my auntie
used to smack me – I used to get the
beating of my life. And the way I
learned how to swim, either you swim
or drown. You know, they just chucked
me in there. When I drowned, they'd
get me out and they'd chuck me back
in again so I'd learn how to swim. It
was horrible. My childhood was really
crap.... My mum married my step-dad –
that's when I fell out badly with me
mum and then I'd unbonded with my
mum because of my step-dad – he hit
me a bit sometimes – my mum wasn't
protecting me or anything like that –
So, I had a really bad childhood.'
(female, aged 15[2])

---

[2] Age at first planned conception.

3

Interpretations and experiences of 'planned' pregnancy

Chapters 3 to 7 will be dedicated to presenting the main findings from the research. Of these, Chapters 3 to 6 will detail findings from the 41 young women interviewed, with Chapter 7 presenting findings from the 10 young men.

As a means of introducing the findings, this chapter looks at the young women's interpretations and experiences of 'planning' their pregnancy. As shown previously, the concept of planning is rather complex and far from a uniform experience. The interviewees ranged from those who scored the highest score on the London Measure of Unplanned Pregnancy (LMUP) questionnaire (the highest degree of planning), to those who were 'positively ambivalent' (those who did not appear to mind whether they became pregnant or not, and were aware of how contraception was used, but were not using it regularly).

Of extreme interest is the fact that, in the interviews with those who at first appeared to be 'positively ambivalent', it often transpired that their planning was actually more definite than their questionnaire suggested. It took some talking and 'warming up' in the interview before some young women felt confident enough to say that they 'planned' their pregnancy. This could be because young women are aware that it is controversial for a young woman to 'plan' a child, and it is a decision that is open to being very negatively judged. As shown in Chapter 2, this was strongly related to age at planned pregnancy. This has implications for tracking surveys such as the British Market Research Bureau survey because, as respondents become older during the course of the survey, the way they respond could change.

There were several different ways in which young women expressed their planning in relation to pregnancy. To illustrate, the following describes how this ranged from clear-cut planning to positive ambivalence towards pregnancy. It is uncertain the extent to which these experiences are unique to the age range that we sampled.

Definitely planning (relatively higher scores on the LMUP questionnaire)

Some young women were very clear about the extent to which their pregnancy was planned. In these cases, the decision was usually talked over together and the couple started 'trying' for a baby. This decision was often taken because the relationship was steady, stable and it seemed like a natural step. This expression of planning seemingly represents a highly rational decision, based on deliberately not using contraception, clear communication between partners and taking steps to foster a healthy pregnancy.

'I was 18, but I was trying for a year and a half – he was very much planned. Yeah – well, I – we first wanted a baby when I was 17, 'cos I been with my husband for – for four and a half years – well, about four years, 'cos I was 16, he was 20. And we decided we wanted a baby quite early on. And we tried for quite a while and it just wasn't happening. And then we stopped trying and then fell pregnant.' (female, aged 18)

'Well, (um) we – we decided and then, like I say, we got [laughs] – we got pregnant like, that first time but (um) like, from the night we decided, I had folic acid and we didn't – I didn't smoke anyway and then we didn't drink, but I didn't really do it for long enough, 'cos I found out like, two weeks later, I was pregnant, so…. [laughs].' (female, aged 18)

A discussion, but limited

For some young women, making the decision to have a baby was conducted without always having a clear or lengthy conversation with their partner. In contrast, it was a topic that seemed to come up naturally when talking about the future, with the discussion usually kept very brief. Some young women report just 'knowing' that they would have a child with their partner, and say that they knew it was just expected that they would. This really illustrates the complexity and degree of uncertainty of how some young women reached this decision. This is interesting, not least because it would be challenging to influence a young woman's decision making through interventions if the actual process of this decision making is unclear.

'We sort of, talked about it – we just didn't – we just – we were just having a conversation of what would happen in the future and we talked about what was gonna happen – it wasn't a set conversation – we just started talking about it.' (female, aged 17)

'It should have been more serious than it was. It was just like, well, I really want a baby and it was me that like, initiated and it and – and then, just tried – we didn't really talk about it much.' (female, aged 17)

'We didn't sit – no – we didn't sit down and say, right, we're gonna have a baby – I think we both knew – it sounds silly, but from when I met him, I knew that it'd happen – I'd only have children with him – obviously we wasn't really using contraception, so

we knew it could happen.' (female, aged 16)

Partner not involved in the planning

Interestingly, for a significant number of interviewees, their partner was not involved in the planning stage of the pregnancy at all. In extreme cases, the partner did not want a child or wanted to wait longer to have a baby, but the young women took over the decision making and stopped taking contraception. More commonly, a male partner would be unsure but the young woman persuaded him or simply stopped talking about it. In these cases where the topic was closed, the male partner would often be aware of the desire for pregnancy although not in total agreement. This has implications for interventions with young men, because it was clear that some young fathers did not feel in control over contraception use and pregnancy planning, and felt it was more the decision and responsibility of their partner.

'Yeah, I wanted to be for ages – oh, well – we both wanted a baby kind of, but he wanted to wait a bit longer – but I just wanted one right now – and I got what I wanted! [laughs]' (female, aged 17)

'It was probably more me – than my partner – it was totally unplanned for my partner – but for me it was probably more, well, we'll see what happens, really.' (female, aged 18)

'Yeah, 'cos he was a bit unsure and (um) but then that like, after a few months of like, thinking about it, he said yeah, I think it is a good idea if we start trying.' (female, aged 16)

Planning for a specific reason

Sometimes the young women planned their pregnancy for a very specific reason. For a small number of young women, this reason was the grief and disappointment of a miscarriage. These interviewees felt the need to plan a baby soon after this, even if the pregnancy that had resulted in miscarriage was not planned.

> 'I think – because we realised the effect of losing the baby had on us, we realised that – you know – we only found out I was pregnant a week or two before it happened, and I was like, oh – I'd really like another baby and M [partner] felt the same. I think M just wanted to make a baby really! [laughs]'. (female, aged 15)

For a small but significant number of interviewees, another very specific reason for 'trying' for a baby was because of the fear of not being able to conceive. There was often a free-floating fear of being infertile, despite being very young and there being no reason to suggest there was a problem. For some, there were actual problems and so planning had taken the form of 'trying', despite knowing that conception may be impossible.

> 'For me, my worst fear was not being able to have a baby, so I wasn't gonna ruin any chance by going on the injection. It [pregnancy] happened early, but that's ok 'cos if I tried to stop it then it might never have happened – and I couldn't handle that.' (female, aged 16)

> 'I thought, well, we might as well try, 'cos my husband's 20 years older than me as well, so – but (um) – yeah – we just thought we'd try, and when we found out about the polycystic ovaries, well, we thought – well, we'll just see if it happens – it happens. If not, it doesn't. Or if it comes to a stage where we really want to, we'll have a look into something else – we'll get help, you see, so....' (female, aged 18)

The following quotation illustrates a young woman worrying about not being able to conceive, for reasons relating to having had her first child at a very young age. This was obviously influential in her planning.

> 'This – (um) with M [baby daughter] she was sort of planned and unplanned, 'cos we wanted to have a baby but it got – we couldn't when we

was trying, so we gave up in the end and I conceived her, so – yeah, 'cos we thought at one stage that none of us could have any more like, could have any kids. And I knew I – I – I had one, and I didn't think that I would be able to have another one – because of having another – having a baby at – at the – age of 12 – 12. G's [partner] motto was, if I got pregnant – and if it happens, it happens – if it don't, it don't – sort of thing, and he's always been like that. I dunno really – I just felt the same as what G has.' (female, age 16)

'Positively ambivalent' (relatively lower scores on the LMUP questionnaire)

As mentioned before, some young women were classed as 'positively ambivalent' about planning their pregnancy. That is, it seemed that they did not mind whether they had a baby or not. Contraception was rarely used, with the young women not caring about avoiding the possibility of pregnancy. Again, in these cases, the decision-making process is not entirely clear. No definite decision was made and no set conversation about having a child took place. It was often left up to chance, commonly expressed as an outcome beyond their control, although with the hope that pregnancy would be the result.

> 'Don't ask me why my body got pregnant – that's up to my body. I wanted a baby, so I was happy, but it was the right time otherwise my body wouldn't have had one.' (female, aged 16)

> 'I think we didn't mind either way – it wasn't like we were really worried – we didn't – we just didn't mind – either – so, if it happened, it happened.' (female, aged 17)

> 'Because I'm not good with regulated, taking pills – and there was times when I'd forget about it and I'd forget about weeks – but we didn't plan it as such, we just thought well, if I stop taking it,

if it happens, it happens – if it doesn't, it doesn't.' (female, aged 18)

''cos we'd just moved in together and – (um) like – I was a bit lazy with the Pill – you know – I didn't – I didn't think, oh – I didn't really think about it – it's hard to – I didn't think, oh, I don't want to have children, or I do wanna have children – I just forgot to take it and then it happened. But if I really didn't want one, I would've been more careful – definitely.' (female, aged 17)

Interestingly, the young women who were classed as 'positively ambivalent' in this study were the ones who displayed tendencies to contradict themselves. On the one hand, they would say they were planning the baby, and then seemed to change and take a fatalistic attitude. This complexity is further illustrated by young women reporting their pregnancy as both planned and unplanned. For these young women, the planning process is possibly the most difficult to unravel.

'I was a bit – you know – I was – I'd been with his dad for about three years, I think, before I got pregnant. I was with him for ages, so I was quite young. I never used precautions, so I s'pose you could say he was planned and not planned really.' (female, aged 16)

These five expressions of pregnancy planning illustrate the different ways in which this was explained by young women. The range in interpretation further illustrates the use of the LMUP questionnaire, where planning is outlined in a scale or continuum rather than a dichotomous expression (that is, planned or 'unplanned' only). A central theme present in most of these examples is how the decision-making processes are far from clear. This has obvious implications for professionals who may be tasked with influencing, or indeed interpreting, such decisions. Also, it was very clear that all young women were very aware about contraception and the mechanisms of how to avoid pregnancy.

To conclude this illustration of planning, it is worth noting three further findings that arose when talking to the young women about when

they first realised they were pregnant. These findings concern their secrecy about planning, the shock of being pregnant, and their strong anti-abortion views.

Secrecy about planning

The fact that the vast majority of interviewees did not tell anyone that their pregnancy was planned is very interesting and telling. Most young women kept this between their partner, close friends and, sometimes, family. They were keen to insist that nobody ever asked them if the baby was planned. It was reported that everyone (friends, family and health professionals) assumed that it was an accident, due to their young age. Because of this, the interviewees reported that it was very easy not to tell people about the planning element, because nobody asked. The reasons for not telling people also centred on not wanting members of their family to be angry and tell them that they had ruined their lives. Through discussion it sometimes became apparent that some of the younger interviewees' pregnancies had been planned more than their questionnaires had indicated.

'He [baby son] was planned (um), but we didn't tell people that it was planned! [laughs] We sort of like, said (um) it was an accident and – you know – just like – well, people just assumed really that it's an accident anyway (um) 'cos you – you're afraid of what – how people react, you know. You – you're a bit worried that they'll be, like – it was pretty much planned but it pretty much seemed like, I think [laughs], more of an accident. But me mum and most people knew that he were planned. But (um) his mum and dad didn't.' (female, aged 18)

'Like, my mum knew me and she knew that I was really mature for my age. My mum took it (um) a lot better but (um) – but nobody really asked, so I didn't actually lie. I didn't turn round and say it was an accident 'cos people just seemed to assume – like y'know – they just assumed.' (female, aged 17)

This illustrates that the young women had a very high awareness of society's negative view of teenage pregnancy and, in particular, planned teenage pregnancy. The fact that the vast majority were not very open about the planning stage, shows that they are worried about being judged and so found it easier and preferable to hide behind the idea that it was accidental. Most reported knowing that their family would stand by them after they found out, but that they would have tried to stop them if they had known at the planning stage. This was also true for telling professionals, and so there are implications for making sexual health support more accessible and non-judgemental. There are many implications for work with young women here.

Shock of being pregnant

Despite the obvious acknowledgement of planning, the majority of young people were evidently shocked at finding out they were pregnant. In explaining this reaction, it should be noted that shock is a common reaction to women of any age when they find out they are pregnant. Indeed, it appears that this 'shock' could be partly explained by impending responsibility, along with actual surprise that pregnancy was the outcome. There could be implications for sex and relationships education here, by emphasising to young people their high levels of fertility.

'I – I was just shocked at first. [Partner] was really pleased. I went and met him in the pub and he got – bought a bottle of champagne and he was quite chuffed about it actually. Yeah – I was – I was after a while. It was a shock at first.' (female, aged 18)

'Oh my God! I'm pregnant! [laughs] It was weird – it was – dunno – felt all funny.... A bit [shocked] because I didn't think I would be pregnant really – not that – that quick.' (female, aged 16)

'I wanted a baby anyway – it was (um) a shock to, to know that I'd fall pregnant that easily, but yeah, I did want a baby and I was very pleased with having that baby.' (female, aged 17)

The notion of 'falling pregnant' implied that for many, stopping the use of contraception was the first stage in planning a baby, and was in no way guaranteed to produce such an immediate outcome. This in itself may be related to the degree of control that young people felt about becoming pregnant, with many young women having a fatalistic view towards the outcome (as illustrated earlier, p 18).

Anti-abortion views

It was very notable that almost all interviewees reported extreme anti-abortion views, and never considered the option of a termination. Such views may support previous research that reports much lower rates of terminations among young women from poorer and deprived areas (Chapter 1). It is evident that the provision of more accessible abortion services in such areas may have little impact on changing this disparity, unless they impact on these very strong beliefs and attitudes. For most, these beliefs were strongly connected to the moral rights of the 'life', and seemed to be deeply entrenched.

''Cos it's a life – I don't – I don't think it's right to kill a life no matter if ... it's just not – don't do it. I'd only do it if I was like – if you get raped ... I just couldn't do it – bring myself to do it.' (female, aged 18)

'I was saying 'Oh I'll have an abortion' – but I knew I couldn't do it ... I don't agree with it at all. It's just wrong and I'd never do it to a baby.' (female, aged 17)

An alternative explanation behind these vehement anti-abortion views could be that they serve as a justification for continuing with a pregnancy, because such strong views are unlikely to be challenged. This explanation is suggested because, often, interviewees could not explain why they held their strong views, despite being asked about religious and spiritual beliefs.

Summary of chapter findings

This chapter has outlined how young women interpreted their pregnancies as planned. The degree of planning ranged across five explanations, from being obvious and clear-cut to 'positive ambivalence' towards falling pregnant. All the young women were aware of available contraception methods , and in no instances was pregnancy the result of an accident or mishap. In order of the highest degree of planning, the five explanations are as follows:

Definitely planned

Clear two-way conversations within a stable relationship, with steps taken to encourage conception and have a healthy pregnancy.

A discussion, but limited

Brief conversation between partners, with more uncertainty towards the decision-making process.

Partner not involved in the planning

Women taking the lead in the decision making with no involvement of partner. Some young fathers reported not feeling in control of the outcome, even if they were aware of their partners' views.

Planning for a specific reason

Reasons were mainly due to the disappointment of a miscarriage or because of the fear of not being able to conceive. There is a need for further research into how feelings of guilt regarding miscarriage could lead to a subsequent planned pregnancy.

'Positively ambivalent'

These young women seemed not to mind whether they became pregnant or not, although were clearly not avoiding the possibility of pregnancy. Pregnancy was often viewed as something beyond their control, although also as a positive outcome.

This chapter also presented three further findings detailing young women's reactions towards pregnancy. First, young women were secretive about the degree of planning and were aware of society's negative view of teenage pregnancy. Second, despite this degree of planning and the awareness of the possibility of becoming pregnant by stopping contraception, young women were still shocked about the outcome. This further illustrated the somewhat fatalistic attitude reported by those who were 'positively ambivalent'. Third, all young women reported strong anti-abortion views, possibly as a means to further justify their choice to become pregnant.

4

Childhood and background influences on 'planned' pregnancy

Having outlined how 'planning' a pregnancy is defined and expressed, it seems logical to move on to how young women's childhood and background experiences influenced this decision. Of the childhood and background factors, there were three leading themes. The first concerns having an unsettled background and the desire for more stability that could be achieved through pregnancy and becoming a parent. Second were young women's negative experiences of school education. Although rarely explicitly stated by the young women themselves, it was obvious that these shared accounts of childhood unsettlement and negative experiences of education played a key role in planning their pregnancies. This was either by providing an impetus towards choosing pregnancy to change their lifecourse, or by their lacking sufficient motivation and desire to actively rule out the possibility of becoming pregnant. The third theme refers to the social and family norms associated with teenage pregnancy in the local vicinity. In the case of this third theme, the quotations are more explicit in reference to choosing pregnancy. Each of these three themes will be outlined in turn.

Theme 1: Unsettled background and a desire for more stability

A very commonly reported explanation for planning to become pregnant was having experienced an unsettled background. Almost all young women reported at least some degree of feeling unsettled while growing up, for various different reasons. Sometimes this unsettled background was due to life events, such as parental separation or divorce, the arrival of a new step-parent, or moving home, area or school. Other times, the unsettled feeling was associated with not feeling secure in their family environment, perhaps due to difficult (and sometimes volatile and violent) family relationships. It was common for young mothers to report that these difficult situations led them into 'trouble', for example, leaving home at an early age, losing direction in life, and generally going 'off the rails'. Each one of the causes of feeling unsettled will now be examined in turn.

Parental separation

Some young women reported that their parents' separation had affected them negatively, made them feel unsettled and often seemed to be a catalyst for further disruptive experiences. Parental separation often led to a new father figure in terms of a step-father, or their mother having a new boyfriend. This was almost always reported as problematic, and most interviewees reported bad family relationships and arguments. In some more serious cases, the situation made the young woman leave home. Leaving home early for these reasons seemed to make the interviewees more vulnerable to further disruption and involvement in risky health behaviours. This is perhaps due to experiencing a lack of parental closeness and guidance. In many cases, their lives were stabilised by meeting a partner, who would ultimately become the father of their child.

'It was very confusing – (um) because my mum and dad split up when I was three-and-a-half, so I sort of, had the heartbreak from there and that sort of, screwed me up a bit – and that's how I became with J [father of baby] – 'cos I was so screwed up, I didn't know where I was going, really.' (female, aged 16)

'I never got on with me step-dad – (um) – I got kicked out of my house – moved up to London and … I got into like, drugs and things like that and I was a bit wild and lots of stuff happened and I couldn't calm myself down – just kept going on the way I was … and got arrested like … and then I started going on the right level and that's when I … I found out I was pregnant.' (female, aged 18)

While some young women recalled the upset of missing their father, others also mentioned that they did not know who their 'real' father was. These distressing experiences were often drawn on when explaining their own choices for parenthood, as a desire for wanting a 'complete' family of their own. Pregnancy offered the young women an opportunity to correct these disruptive and unstable experiences, and enable them to focus their attention on ensuring this would not happen in their own parent–child dynamic.

'I do know who he is – I know his name and I know where he's living, but I – I don't know what to believe. I don't know whether – I don't know whether to go and find him or just leave it the way it is, because if it is true, what my mum was saying – about my dad leaving me – and not – not wanting me – then it would be better off if I didn't know him…. I just wanted better than that for my children.' (female, aged 17)

Difficult relationships within the family (including violence)

The data from interviewees showed that some young women had experienced physical and sexual violence while growing up, either in the family or towards them personally. The number of interviewees reporting such experiences was more frequent than expected, with a significant proportion reporting physical and sexual abuse. These situations often led the young woman to feel depressed and distant from her family. It generally led to problems at school, sometimes leaving home early, meeting the father of her child, wanting something better for her own child, and becoming pregnant.

'It wasn't a great family life! [laughs] Wasn't a great childhood. [laughs] It was great in some ways but (um) I ended up (um) being sexually abused, so it wasn't good in another way [laughs] … It was one of my brothers, so … it was just (um) getting too much – I was like, really depressed so I just had to drop out [of school] because I was like, killing myself, healthwise.' (female, aged 17)

'I got sexually abused by my step-dad. And I got beaten up by my step-dad and I got sexually abused by my mum…. That's when I told my teacher and they kicked me out…. It hurt – it really hurt. It's like, knowing my own mother could do something like that, but (um) I've just had to – I've learned how to cope with it all now. And I – I'm better off without 'em – I know I am. 'Cos they're all – they're alcoholics and they're druggies as well. They do the needles and that lot … the reason why I wouldn't ever inject is because of my mum trying to stab me with a used, like, needle.' (female, aged 17)

Moving location frequently

Many young women reported moving location frequently when growing up. Not only was the area new, but this also usually meant starting a new school and making new friends. The move was often due to changing family circumstances (for example, new step-parent or mother's boyfriend). Recollections by interviewees all pointed to the fact that this was usually a very unsettling experience although, in some cases, the move was because the new area was deemed preferable by their parents. This was often reported by the young women as distressing, and some reported this change leading to loss of friends, depression and generally feeling unsettled.

'I – when my mum had a boyfriend, he – she – we lived in [name of town]…. And he had a daughter and she was very much into drugs and stuff … we didn't get on very well, so I moved in with my grandma, and I kept doing that, several times, throughout my life…. I think the school kind of, knew I had a bit of a dysfunctional life…. We lived in one, two, three – four houses with my mum and my step-dad, but I've always – my mum's had really itchy feet – she can't stay in one house too long.' (female, aged 19)

'We used to live with my dad, up at [name of road], and they sold that and my – like, when my mum and dad got divorced … (um) we just sort of – mum sold the house and we split it and we sort of like, moved on then. And we moved to another house and my mum met someone else, so we moved in with him, and then we all moved up here and then, now they've broke up and – [laughs]' (female, aged 16)

Theme 2: Negative experiences of school education

The young women reported shared attitudes and experiences towards their school education. Almost all the young women talked about their school days in a negative manner. This was illustrated by recalling negative experiences, such as dislike towards the work and teachers, the effects of bullying and the desire to truant. Ultimately, many reported poor educational attainment and a lack of direction or an alternative lifecourse besides parenthood. These themes will be detailed in turn.

Dissatisfaction with school work and teachers

The majority of interviewees had little or no interest in the work at school, and frequently described it as 'boring' and 'pointless'. Nobody recalled anything being done to make the work more interesting, and many saw school as a 'laugh' and did not take it seriously.

'I didn't really like, pay much attention in school … I didn't – didn't do any of my GCSEs or anything. I took school as a bit of – just, messing around and that really! [laughs] Didn't do much work!' (female, aged 17)

'It was ok – some lessons I thought were rubbish – I didn't see the point in going, but school was good – it was – it was a laugh.' (female, aged 14)

Most expressed regret at not finishing school and not doing their GCSEs. However, although most admitted being very 'difficult' pupils, some now felt angry that they were discouraged to become engaged in school work, either through the school system or by their family. There was a sense of having 'missed out' on education, and having to live with that lost opportunity, because they did not realise the importance of education while at school.

'Nobody made me go [to school]. A welfare officer came round for a while, but they gave up on me pretty quickly. Maybe they should've tried a bit harder to get me to go, 'cos now I can't get a job that I wanna do, but I didn't really get that at the time.' (female, aged 15)

'I could of done a lot better … I don't think my mum – my dad sort of, would say oh, yeah – yeah – I want the best for you … my mum was like, 'Just go to school'. She didn't really like, ask for homework and stuff – to see like, when it wasn't done. Kind of, she didn't ask me if it had been done or anything like that. So – I don't think she supported us – or me – she's better now [laughs] – but she didn't.' (female, aged 17)

A further common experience of education was the dislike of teachers. The reasons reported were sometimes because they felt 'picked on', but mainly because of their general dislike of being told what to do. This could indicate that the young women in this sample found it difficult to relate to teachers and the school environment. Perhaps they had a rebellious aspect to their personality which meant that, consciously or unconsciously, they were finding a way to take control of their lives by disengaging with school.

'Some teachers were ok – other teachers I used to swear at – I didn't like them at all. I spent a lot of Year 10 excluded.' (female, aged 14)

'I went to an old-fashioned school, with the blazers and the ties – and all the teachers made you stand up when they walked in the room. Now, that should be fine, but I found that personally – why should I stand up? I don't stand up for my parents, so why am I gonna stand up for them? It was a – very much, you're the child, I'm the teacher.' (female, aged 17)

Bullying and truancy

A further dislike of school was made in relation to being bullied. When this was discussed during the interview, it was clear that many interviewees still found this an upsetting subject to recall, as it was associated with painful memories of loneliness, exclusion, truanting, getting into trouble (for example, alcohol and/or drugs), and sometimes self-harm.

'It was verbal, it was physical – she used to smash my face into brick walls – she used to humiliate me … and kick me and punch me and get all her friends to pin me back and things like that. But I was too weak 'cos I was only about six stone by then – I – I couldn't do anything … when you get bullied as bad as I did, you used to do things to make sure you didn't go to school. I used to tip orange – apple juice in my bed to make it look like I'd wet myself so I didn't have to go to school and I had an infection or I'd make up some story … they offered for me to study in a private room but I said 'no' and just left.' (female, aged 18)

'I was bullied really badly and I just didn't go to school. I missed about two years. I ended up drinking and taking speed like, every day for about a year. I cut my wrists and took overdose – my aunty found me and took me to hospital … I didn't actually want to kill myself, though. When I went back it was ok, but I never really knew what I was doing and so I only came out with two GCSEs in the end.' (female, aged 17)

Collectively, the apparent dislike of school and experiences of bullying was often behind the truanting from school reported by many of the young women. Problems were further exacerbated by the truanting leading to formal exclusion from school.

'I got – I got kicked out in the last year…. Just messing around with everyone at school – so we all got kicked out…. Just stupid things really. Throwing things in the classroom and stuff [laughs] – and not going to school.' (female, aged 18)

'My step-dad and my mum used to drop me off at that gate, and I used to go in, come back out – like, when they had drove off – and light a fag, and walk off – and go and skive off [laughs] for the day! I was terrible! … I used to play like, football down at the estate [laughs] … And I used to get caught every tim…. Yeah – but all my friends skived off with me. [laughs] And they've all – half of them have got babies now as well! [laughs] … I dunno. I was just more interested in smoking and going down town with the boys and having a drink, than going to school. School was boring. [laughs]' (female, aged 16)

Although these negative experiences and dislike of school were implicit in young women's decisions to become pregnant, there were isolated cases of where a causal link was more evident. For most, dissatisfaction with school contributed to the desire to become pregnant. However, the following person reports that her dislike of school was seemingly *due* to the fact she wanted to become pregnant (although the extent to which school may have been used as a reason, or even an excuse, for becoming pregnant is questionable):

'I just didn't like school – I (um) – I hated it. I hated being there. I didn't like the people there – I (um) – I hated it, I really hated it … I just hated that environment – I hated being there – I just (um) – it was horrible. I would just rather have been out doing other things! [laughs] Working even or – you know – doing stuff at home … I just didn't like going to school.… Like, one: I didn't wanna go to school, and two: I was just determined to have a baby. I was just gonna have one – it was gonna happen.' (female, aged 13)

Poor educational attainment and direction

The apparent dislike of school, bullying and non-attendance experienced by many of our sample ultimately resulted in poor educational attainment. Many of the sample took no GCSEs and, for those who did, few passes were reported. This poor educational attainment led to growing perceptions about limited life-options regarding further education and/or employment. Indeed, some young women reported that they did not know what else they could do, and so having a baby seemed like a positive decision. Many interviewees did not want to do a 'boring' or mundane job with no direction, meaning or room to progress. This led them to choose to have a baby instead, possibly to give them a real sense of purpose in life and some future direction. The quotations taken from the transcripts are particularly striking as they illustrate, quite explicitly, how this aspect of their childhood influenced their choice to plan a pregnancy in their teenage years.

'I wasn't bothered [about planning to be pregnant] 'cos it – 'cos I – I didn't know what I wanted to do after school, and then I just got a job 'cos I didn't know what I wanted to do, and then like, I met me partner and had K [baby], so like, nothing really developed out of my GCSEs.' (female, aged 17)

'Obviously, if I'd got the results that I'd wanted when I was at school, I wouldn't of had children so young, but I think I wasn't doing a lot else at that time, and I thought, oh, you know, I – 'cos I always knew I wanted to have children – I thought if I do have children – and 'cos I met S [partner] you know … I thought, oh, I could do all that now and have my career later – what's the point of waiting, really – you know … I think I was just bored before – I know it sounds strange but I was just working, and we'd get home and we'd both just like, sit there, 'cos we didn't wanna go out or anything and so – yeah – bored! [laughs] … yeah – definitely. I think 'cos I'd had this purpose like, you know, going to school and everything … and then all of a sudden, there was nothing and I was just working and – yeah – it was, sort of, what's the point of this – you know – how long are we gonna carry this on for, you know? [laughs] … I just think it was like, a time in my life when I didn't – didn't have anything else to do, you know? And I thought, you know, I'm with the right person and it feels right to do it now, even though he didn't come out and say let's have a baby together, but I knew he would be fine about it as well.' (female, aged 19)

Theme 3: Social and family norms in the local area

The young women's own childhood and background experiences had also shaped their views towards teenage pregnancy as a life-choice. In drawing reference to the local vicinity and neighbourhood, it was very common for the young women to report being surrounded by a norm of settling down early. Therefore, for most, becoming pregnant appeared to be a normal lifecourse, and there was no likelihood of any recrimination or negative judgement over their decision. With so many young mothers visible in their world, the local vicinity was perceived to be very accommodating and supportive of their choice. This was reported very frequently, and the vast majority of the interviewees were comfortable with their decision to become pregnant.

'Nobody ever bats an eyelid about it – they'd be doing it all day round here if they were bothered! I don't care anyway – I'm not too young. I'm young – but it's not about age and I do believe that.' (female, aged 16)

In view of the more immediate family, the fact that most interviewees' mothers were full-time mothers reinforced the normality of teenage pregnancy. For many, their own parents were pregnant as teenagers themselves and had followed the same lifecourse.

'I always wanted to do just what my mum did – it worked for her! She never wanted anything else, and that was the same for me. It's hard, but she's a good baby and I'd rather do this all day than work – well, it's still working but y'know what I mean.' (female, aged 15)

'My mum's never had a job – she just had me and my sisters – like, quite young. Like, a housewife-type thing. And that's what all my friends' mums are too. There's tons of teenage mums round here – I don't know why – nobody looks at me funny 'cos there's so many of us. [laughs]' (female, aged 17)

In our study it was found that the majority of the young women were fairly happy with their situation, and did not see anything 'wrong' with being a young mother. Most wished that they had more money to buy things for their child, but they were generally fairly content with their lives, the area they lived in, and being a teenage mother. This could be because the normality and security of living somewhere they were accustomed to was important to them. Most young women had family living close by, and spoke of the security this provided.

'I haven't got loads, but there are people worse than me. We do all right, and I think – well, everyone says – I do fine. It's all right round here, and I think I'm really lucky really. I wouldn't want to be nowhere else, 'cos my mum's over the road.' (female, aged 15)

'There's things I need, and I do struggle sometimes but – at the end of the day – I've got a child who loves me and I love my child. I know it'll be all right, and I wouldn't change my life at all – not at all. I know people, and I've got friends – it's a friendly place.' (female, aged 16)

'I know about this area, and I know they're always trying to do stuff to make it better – but it isn't ever gonna change. But, you're ok if you know people, and my family have been here for years so it's ok – we'll always be ok.' (female, aged 18)

Summary of chapter findings

Although not always stated explicitly, it was clear that the young women's childhood and background had, in some way, provided a foundation for their decision to become pregnant. The key point raised through this chapter was that choosing to become pregnant was perceived to 'correct' their deprived childhood and alter their lifecourse for the better. The young women spoke candidly about their unsettled background, their dissatisfaction and various problems associated with school. This was in stark contrast to the sense of purpose and future associated with their child. Their childhood and background experiences within the local neighbourhood and immediate family had also impressed on young people that teenage pregnancy was very much a 'normal' lifecourse.

The experiences reported suggest that these are vulnerable young women whose experiences while growing up led them to actively plan a pregnancy, or at least not take any measures to avoid one. From the array of experiences described, they were classified into three main themes of explanation:

Unsettled background and a desire for more stability, due to:

1. Parental separation:
   This was very common, and was reported as very unsettling for many. The lack of a father figure was evident in some interviewees planning to have their own 'proper' family.
2. Difficult relationships within the family (including violence):
   Many young women had experienced feeling unsettled due to negative and volatile relationships within the family, leading to a lack of parental closeness and security and a desire to leave, settle down and have a 'better' family of their own.
3. Moving location frequently:
   This was reported as very unsettling, and often led to disengaging with existing friends, going 'off the rails', and losing interest in school.

Negative experiences of school education, due to:

1. Dissatisfaction with work and teachers:
   The majority of interviewees disliked or even hated academic work, and wanted to leave school. There were also frequent clashes with teachers, also causing disengagement.
2. Bullying and truancy:
   Bullying was a main cause of truanting, depression, self-harm and extreme disengagement with school.
3. Poor educational attainment and direction:
   The ultimate outcome following the negative experiences of school was poor educational attainment. Due to the perceived limited life options, in terms of further education or meaningful employment, this was commonly reported as a reason for planning a pregnancy.

Social and family norms

Childhood and background experiences from the local neighbourhood and immediate family highlighted the normality of becoming pregnant as a teenager. Teenage parents were most visible in these environments, which tended to support young people's decisions over pregnancy. Their own childhood experiences of being brought up by a teenage parent(s) had also fostered support over this lifecourse. However, it is interesting to note the apparent contradiction, because many young women hid the fact they were planning a child, despite this perceived normality.

5

Individual needs and preferences for 'planned' pregnancy

This chapter expands on the childhood and background factors outlined in Chapter 4. In contrast to the earlier reported findings, many of the themes presented here illustrate more clearly *how* the young mothers' own background impacted on their motivations towards pregnancy. Consequently, the findings and quotations presented are more explicit and direct in explaining these motivations. These explanations have been defined as young women's 'need' for an alternative lifecourse and positive preferences for parenthood.

These two explanations are separated thematically, because they are deemed to be very different. Young women felt a need for an alternative lifecourse more strongly, and saw this as the driving force behind planning a baby. These needs were normally related to negative situations or insecurities (including those faced during their childhood) that the young women intended to escape from. In short, it was perceived that pregnancy offered them an alternative, and more preferable, a lifecourse with the chance of gaining a new sense of identity. On the other hand, the positive preferences for parenthood were less related to any negative experiences faced during their own childhood and background. As such, young women's positive preferences for parenthood are likely to be similar to reasons offered by many older women, without the background of disadvantage.

Theme 1: The need for an alternative lifecourse

These needs were divided into four sub-themes as follows:

To escape home life

Many interviewees were living in different accommodation, away from their childhood home, as a result of having a child. Some of the younger women (14- and 15-year-olds) were still living at their family home, but most were living in local authority (temporary or permanent) accommodation with or without their partner. This accommodation was provided for them primarily because of their teenage pregnancy.

A small yet significant minority of interviewees reported that part of their reason for planning their pregnancy was to gain a route out of the family home and live independently. This need to get out of this environment was due to many of the background factors reported in Chapter 4 (such as a volatile home environment). This is a controversial point, as it has often been reported that this could be the most prolific reason for teenage pregnancy (that is, young women plan to become pregnant to get a local authority house of their own). However, this was only reported by a small number of interviewees and, even in these cases, was perceived more of an escape route than wanting their own home per se.

'Housing-wise – in a way we're better off because we're living by ourselves, but also, when we did live – 'cos we basically lived with my mum for a while – you know … she was in all day, every day – so, in – but it wasn't ours, whereas this is ours. We're responsible for paying the – the rent every week [laughs] – we're responsible for putting food in the cupboard, you know – and that's what I dreamed of really. Having a baby and getting out of that situation with my mum's drinking.' (female, aged 16)

Need for their own loving family

A key reason for young women planning to become pregnant was the desire to have a loving family of their own. A very high proportion of interviewees cited this as their main motivation, and their reasons for wanting this at a young age were again very much tied in with their unsettled and negative background experiences (see Chapter 4). In contrast to their own childhood, young women spoke about wanting to feel loved and wanting to care for a child. A desire for unconditional love and the feeling of being needed was frequently mentioned. The young women frequently reported craving the feeling of being needed and loved by a child, who represented something new and not related to their family and past events and problems.

'I – I had a really, really bad childhood – like, (um) I was in care and I – I just – 'cos my parents aren't very good parents [laughs] so – and (um) I – I just thought a baby would give me that stability and also give me something that would love me unconditionally – you know – never thought it would leave me and – 'cos it'd be mine – nobody could take it away or – and it would be mine … I was the only kid at the age of nine, planning to have a baby…. Like, my destiny … I had my baby that I wanted – I – you know, I wanted B [baby son] – I was desperate for B and I had him, and I – I've enjoyed him so much.' (female, aged 13)

'Maybe it's just – yeah, because maybe just – might be (um) – it just feels great when – when like, you've got a child who just – you know – following you around, telling you they love you and I think that's – it is quite selfish, but that's one of the reasons why I became a mum because I wanted someone who'll – you know – love 'em to bits 'cos it's not just your child who's the centre of your world – the parents are the centre of the child's world, and that feels great as well, so I think – yeah – yeah, that's – that's – it's brilliant. It is fantastic because – you know – they're – the child's dependent on you and you know that (um) – that you – if you – you know – you've gotta do everything for the child and it just feels great to be depended on.' (female, aged 17)

Gaining a purpose to their life

It was very common for the young women to report a sense of worthlessness prior to becoming pregnant. These young women reported feeling empty, unhappy and bored. They felt a need to do something with their life, and they perceived motherhood as a preferred lifecourse. They reported feeling that coming home every evening after a day in a 'dead-end' job was boring and pointless. This point clearly ties in with poor educational experiences and attainment (Chapter 4), showing that pregnancy and parenthood offered an alternative purpose in life and an opportunity to find a new sense of identity.

'Because I was so unhappy – I was so – you know – so unhappy. I didn't have a place for anything. I hated school, I didn't – I didn't have anything (um) and B [baby son] gave me that – B gave me my purpose and my place in life, and my goal.' (female, aged 13)

''Cos I wanted children [laughs] – and I wasn't – you know – doing anything else really – I wasn't working and – so it wasn't – nothing just – nothing getting in the way really – apart from my mum, but she was really, really happy anyway, so – I was, like, lost – I didn't know what to do with myself, 'cos I was just working and thinking, this is pointless – I'm not enjoying this, or I'm not enjoying what I'm doing at the moment.' (female, aged 19)

This feeling of worthlessness was also associated with the area where they were living, or had lived when they were growing up. This was usually because it was a relatively deprived area, with a lack of jobs and careers to aspire to.

'What can you do when you grow up round here anyway? There's too many kids going to school and then nothing for them to do. There's no decent jobs, and then they wonder why girls get pregnant. For me it was because I wanted to do something – I wasn't gonna do nothing, like, so that's like, that's like my job – being a mum to K [baby son]. If you know what I mean.' (female, aged 17)

'Nobody ever said anything to me at school – like – do you wanna do such-and-such a job … everyone knows you probably couldn't do them types of things round here so maybe that's why they don't put it in your head in the first place! [laughs] You'd only be pissed off that you couldn't do it, wouldn't ya. I see being a mum as a job though … if I didn't, if I wasn't a mum I don't think I'd even have a job, so it was probably a good decision for me – personally.' (female, aged 18)

In relation to this, some young people reported a history of unemployment in their family and, therefore, they expressed a feeling that there was no point in trying to have a career because there were no jobs. This could be a learnt acceptance, handed down through generations of unemployment and disillusionment.

'She [mother] did have a job, I think, but it closed or something. My dad worked, and that was it – it was just up to him really 'cos I don't, well I don't know what she could've done. It's just jobs for men round here really and not many either … places close down and you have to go a good few miles out to get a job. And there's not much point 'cos you don't get much anyway – and it's bad hours.' (female, aged 16)

These lack of alternative options and opportunities were particularly evident among those young women interviewed in more rural, isolated locations. For these young women, becoming pregnant to gain a purpose in their life was especially striking. Young women in these locations reported that prior to becoming pregnant, they experienced practical barriers to going to college, or going further afield for a job that was better-paid with better prospects.

The main barrier to post-16 studying or employment for these women was the lack of affordable transport. The nearest college and town were often a few miles away and, without a car, this was impossible for most. Before having a baby, this meant that college was a very difficult option. The following interviewee actually jokes that the reason why she and so many of her peers became young parents was because of the barriers to getting to college.

'I wanted to do interior design, but I had to go away to [name of town]. It was really far for me to go – I just couldn't fit it all in, and it was really expensive – so I'll wait 'til she's [baby daughter] at school and then I'll probably do it – 'cos it'll be a bit easier then. I think it should have been easier to go, 'cos all my friends wanted to go and we couldn't, and now most of us have got babies. What does that say? [laughs]' (female, aged 17)

After having a baby, this problem was still the same with the added disadvantage that the journey increased the amount of time spent away from their baby. This also increased child-minding fees greatly, making it an impossible option. Therefore, further education was also cut off from these young women after becoming a mother.

'I'd never be back in time for him [baby son], and I'm on my own so nobody could take him. So, with money and travel and everything, I can't do it [college] now, so I'll have to wait 'til he's older maybe – if I've got any more money in a few years – probably not though. [laughs]' (female, aged 16)

Desire to prove capability

Young women also reported how choosing to become pregnant allowed them to prove to themselves and others that they were capable of bringing up a child. For many, this demonstration of capability was a means of putting their own childhood experiences behind them, by proving that they could do a better job of having a child and bringing up a family than their own parents did. They wanted their child to have a better experience of growing up feeling loved, wanted, cared for and supported, with two parents, a stable life and sufficient money. This strong need to change things was realised by planning a baby early in life. Often, the young women who had experienced unsettled backgrounds had matured and grown up relatively quickly, and so felt ready to take on the responsibility of a baby despite what anyone might think of them becoming a young mother.

> 'I wanted her [baby daughter] to have a better childhood than what I had, which she's getting, 'cos if I didn't give her what she – wants, then I – there wouldn't be nothing for me to have her because I would just be like my mum, and I wouldn't like that … she didn't ask to be brought into this world and have to go through the same thing as what I've been through.' (female, aged 11)

> 'I wanted to give him [baby son] – give him stability – in a stable home and like, just – just live a life that was – the stability – everything that I didn't have – it was just – I really, really wanted to give everything for him – just a stable home, a really nice life – and he – and he's got that.' (female, aged 13)

Theme 2: Positive preferences for parenthood

These positive preferences for parenthood were oriented around two explanations as follows:

A love of babies, and experience of caring for them

The vast majority of young women already had a significant amount of experience with babies and/or young children before they became pregnant. Being involved and surrounded by babies made them realise how much they enjoyed looking after them. This led many of the young women to want a child of their own, perhaps earlier than their peers would be considering it, partly because they felt capable and comfortable in the maternal role.

> ''Cos I got loads of little brothers and I always used to look after them – so I thought it would be fun to have my own! [laughs]' (female, aged 18)

> 'I've had a lot of things – experience with kids. I baby-sat all the time … everybody said I'd be a good mum, the amount of children I'd looked after, and I knew exactly what I was doing when I got pregnant.' (female, aged 18)

> 'My mum's – from being – as long as I can remember, she's been a childminder … my house was always full of children and (um) I used to go down to the playgroup all summer holidays and help there, so like, I was kind of like, like – (um) I had a lot of experience with children and I loved doing things … it's funny, when you're a really little girl, you'll say – oh, (um) you know, I wanna have babies at this age and get married at this age [laughs], and so I did.' (female, aged 18)

Partly as a consequence of this early experience of looking after young children, the vast majority of young women stated that they had always wanted a job in childcare. For most, however, difficulties were faced in training for such a career. Therefore, becoming a mother, in a sense, provided a similar but more viable option.

'I wanted to be a teacher – [laughs] and (um) – I just always wanted to be with kids, always and (um) – but a mum, definitely, yeah.' (female, aged 13)

'All I wanted to do was be a nursery nurse or a childminder, but now I've looked into doing midwifery – that's what I'd like to do when he's [baby son] is a bit older – I really want to be a midwife.' (female, aged 17)

Several of the young women reported having responsibility for the care of younger siblings in the past. This increased responsibility may have been due to problems in the family, such as parental alcohol abuse, or long-term illness. This frequently caused school to be missed, which, in turn, often led to disengagement and subsequent problems such as falling behind with academic work and losing friends.

'When I was six years old, I was sitting at home looking after my sister, which is – she's 12 now – (um) 'cos my mum couldn't cope. I had to get up with her during the night and feed her, bath her, change her – I had to do all of the stuff that a real mother would do.' (female, aged 11)

'My mum isn't what you'd call a confident person, and she couldn't cope with us. I missed two years of school 'cos I was off looking after her [younger sister], 'cos I was like her mum really. I did everything for her and now I'm gone I worry that she's not ok – not being looked after and that.' (female, aged 16)

'I've grown up around lots of kids, 'cos I'm the – I'm the – I'm the third oldest, so I've grown up around loads of little babies, so I'm basically – I'm – I've always had a thing for little babies … 'cos my mum was in and out of – 'cos my mum was in and out of hospital quite a lot, (um) 'cos of her epilepsy, and my – my dad was like, with his girlfriend. Obviously, they did – they did come out and look after us, but

there was lots of time where I – I was like, looking after my younger brothers and I just got used to it.' (female, aged 18)

To 'get it over with young'

It was very common for the young women to report their motivations for planning a pregnancy as not wanting to be an 'old' parent. The majority of interviewees reported wanting to have a baby at a young age, so that they were still young enough to enjoy them, keep up with them, and be closer in age to make the parent–child relationship easier.

'I always thought that I wouldn't wanna leave it too long – you're meant to have easier labours. I don't know how true that is yet – but! [laughs] – [long pause] – it's not so much of a generation gap, and you sort of, know – sort of, see their point of view more.' (female, aged 16)

'I wanted a baby quite young 'cos then I can go out with her when she's older and so I won't be too old! [laughs]' (female, aged 18)

Another very common reason for choosing motherhood early was so that they could 'get on with their life', for financial and career reasons. It was widely believed that, after a couple of years, they would be able to pursue other options and, in a sense, get their original life back as having children was 'out of the way'. Although this could be construed as an inaccurate perception of the future (see Chapter 6), it was often cited as a reason for choosing young motherhood as opposed to waiting until later in life.

'It sounds really awful, but so that I can get on with my life. You know – in a way, if you like, [laughs] get them out of the way! [laughs] Because I had T [baby son], if I wanted to have any more – then I can carry on with my life, 'cos – and also, I just think we were both ready for another one, and it was financially better as well, 'cos we had all of our stuff from T – we could – you know – so – especially when we found out he was a boy, it was brilliant.' (female, aged 16)

'I do think like, once – like, if like, in a good few years, we can start getting our life back. We – we – we can – 'cos there's no – I don't think there's any point now, in waiting another 10 years to have another kid because then we're starting from the beginning again. So, like, I think it's better if we're gonna have the kids we want, have 'em in – within the next like, five years, and then in 10 years or so, we'll have our lives back. We'll – we'll be able to do what we want, when we want, really.' (female, aged 17)

Summary of chapter findings

It is clear that the young women's individual need for an alternative lifecourse and positive preferences for parenthood have been influential in the planning of their pregnancy. As noted in Chapter 4, the young women did not always make clear the causal links between their childhood and background experiences, and planning a baby. However, in this chapter, much stronger and clearer causal links can be seen. The key point raised here was that young women often planned a pregnancy because of a need to escape a negative situation. It was often perceived as a viable route out of an unhappy home, or a boring situation and an opportunity for a new sense of identity. It was also very common for young women to perceive a need to prove to others that they could do something on their own. This seemed to stem from insecurity, and a feeling of worthlessness.

In addition, young women also reported more positive, and possibly more acceptable reasons for choosing young motherhood. It is likely that the themes categorised as positive preferences would be relevant for all parents, irrespective of their age, or background circumstances.

The need for an alternative lifecourse

1. To escape home life:
   A small, yet significant, number of young women reported a need to escape from a current negative situation at home. It was felt that a child would give them the freedom to leave and start a new life. However, becoming pregnant to 'get a house' per se was rarely given as a reason. Nevertheless, it is possible that the young women were aware of society's views about this, and so felt reluctant to give this as a reason for planning.
2. Need for a 'proper' and loving family of one's own:
   The majority of interviewees reported a need for their own family, which tied in with wanting to escape a negative home life. There was a clear 'need' for something new and more positive in their life. A need to be loved unconditionally was also frequently given as a reason.
3. Gaining a purpose to their life:
   As a means to escape boredom and to fill an apparent void in their life, some young women chose pregnancy as a means to change their lifecourse, and give their own existence a sense of purpose and identity. High levels of deprivation, exacerbated in rural locations, provided limited life-options. Having a child was an easier means of feeling worthwhile than education or gaining a career.
4. Desire to prove capability:
   Background factors often led to low self-esteem, and many young women reported a need to prove their capability by doing something independently. Motivations were centred around being a more capable parent than their own.

Positive preferences for parenthood

1. A love of babies, and experience of caring for them:
   Most young women reported always having a great affection and love for babies and children. Thus, some recalled either wanting to work with them, or have their own, from a very young age. For many, having their own children was easier than gaining careers in childcare. Many felt confidence in their ability, due to having had a significant

amount of experience of childcare within the family.

2. To 'get it over with young':
   On a more practical note, some interviewees expressed a preference for having babies young so that they would still have time to enjoy their lives and do other things. Several spoke about wanting to avoid a big age gap that may hamper parent–child communication and relations.

It is important to highlight that a theme central to this and the previous chapter has been the local vicinity or area. The interviews clearly showed how poor and disadvantaged geographical areas were more prone to teenage pregnancy (although we must acknowledge that we did not interview a control group of young mums in less deprived areas). It appears that three features of the local area may explain the higher prevalence of planned pregnancy. First, an area that is relatively deprived presents a perceived lack of employment or training opportunities. Pregnancy and parenthood, in contrast, offer young women an alternative and meaningful lifecourse, and an option that is fully in their control. Second, the lack of opportunities is exacerbated in rural locations where accessibility to employment, further education and training are further hindered by the expense and availability of transport. Third, and arguably most powerful of all, evidence of teenage parenthood in these areas demonstrates its normality (a point raised in Chapter 4). The high visibility of young mums in these areas illustrates the acceptance of teenage pregnancy, and further demonstrates it as a viable option in life.

As a final point, given the disadvantaged childhood and background circumstances common to the majority of our sample, the decisions to become a teenage parent appear reasonably rational. Pregnancy and parenthood offer these young women a chance to change their lives for the better. Unlike most alternative ways of changing their life, such as education, training or employment, pregnancy is an option which is perceived as totally within their own control. In reflection, the vast majority were adamant that pregnancy had been the right decision at this time in their life. Chapter 6, comparing young women's lives pre- and post-pregnancy, will explore this point further.

6

Reflecting on pregnancy

This chapter takes the subject of 'planning' a pregnancy to another stage. It presents findings from those young women who were asked to reflect, as young parents, on their earlier decision to plan their pregnancy. It examines the young women's current perceptions of how becoming a young parent has affected them. Most young women reported very positive experiences of being a mum, and seem to believe wholeheartedly that they made the right decision. However, as a note of caution, it could be said that some young women feel a sense of having to justify their decision to plan a baby. Also, it is very possible that many mothers would not feel comfortable saying that they regret their decision to have their baby, because it could appear that their child is unwanted. Also, it needs to be recognised that the influence of the partner and the acceptance by family members appears influential in these young women's accounts. The analysis excludes the seven women who were pregnant at the time of interview.

Reasons for feeling pleased with the decision to 'plan' a child and reasons for feeling regret are separated thematically in this chapter. It should be noted from the start that the latter was not reported as often as the former. Two contrasting case studies will be added to illustrate the different themes. It is also important to state that these reflections were from women who had a child less than one year of age. It may be the case that accounts could differ from those with children beyond this age.

Theme 1: Pleased with the decision to plan pregnancy

The positive reflections on planning a pregnancy are categorised as a general sense of happiness and fulfilment, and improved finances and housing. Both are outlined in turn.

Happiness and fullfilment

Confidence and fulfilment

Most of the young women interviewed reported feeling happier now than before they became pregnant. Feeling 'fulfilled' and more confident was frequently reported. It was apparent that the young women felt a sense of having a new purpose and a role in life, that they felt was lacking before. Many interviewees reported that their baby had given them a new-found confidence that they really appreciated and enjoyed. For finances and housing, this effect of being a young parent was not always cited as a reason. Feeling this way was a positive outcome that was not anticipated at the time of planning.

'I used to think life was crap [laughs] until I had C [baby son].' (female, aged 16)

'Before I was really low because I wasn't doing anything I wanted to do and now – I don't know – she just seems to bring a lot of confidence to me and I'm proud of her because she's a gorgeous baby and she does lots of things – and – yeah, I'm a lot happier than I was before, but I think before I was really, really low.' (female, aged 18)

'Because I would not change her for anything. [laughs] I'm so glad that she's here – she's like, totally changed my – and she's given me more confidence as well. I was like – before, I was very shy – I wouldn't even probably go into a shop and ask for something – with her – she's like a barrier there – she like, gives me the confidence – I'm saying, this is me – this is my baby – and I'm gonna go in there and do that, and it's like really – it's much better.' (female, aged 17)

Many young women said that they did not miss their old life, in particular going out with their friends. Many admitted to having changed, and liking different things (in other words, staying in with their family). It was clear that, for many interviewees, having a child had changed them significantly and led to a new maturity.

'All my mates said – that lot said – because of her, I'm giving up my whole life, basically. But I'm not, 'cos it's just a new beginning. I'm not bothered about going out partying, going out clubbing, and that lot, to be honest. I'd rather sit at home with my family ... I think the only thing that I would miss out on was her – if I had – if I was to go out and – go out partying and that – I'd always miss her. I'm not bothered whether I go out or not no more.' (female, aged 17)

Closer family relationships

Perhaps unsurprisingly, most young women considered that having a child had brought them closer to their family. The young women who had experienced negative relationships with their family saw this as especially positive. They saw having a child as bringing the family closer again, because everyone loved the baby, despite not approving of the pregnancy initially. Again, this was rarely cited as an actual reason for planning a pregnancy, but was seen as a very positive effect.

'I go and see her [interviewee's mother] quite often – but it's really weird because like – like, my mum is totally like, not maternal [laughs] but now S [baby daughter] is here, she just absolutely loves her – you know – it's really strange to see my mum that way, but it's definitely made us closer.' (female, aged 18)

'He [interviewee's father] wasn't as sure when I first – he was like, are you sure you want the baby? – and all that – 'cos I suppose I was young at the time – pregnant at 17. But I was like, yeah, I'm keeping it whether you like it or not sort of thing – now he just loves him to bits. He wants me to go along there like, every day to see him, sort of thing! [laughs] He's [baby son] brought us a lot closer as father and daughter.' (female, aged 17)

A 'new' life

When the young women were asked to reflect on their decisions around pregnancy, the majority thought their life would be worse if they had not become a parent. The young women who had experienced problems with drugs, alcohol and crime prior to pregnancy were more likely to give this response. They viewed becoming a mother as a positive step that meant they were not getting into trouble anymore. Some thought their behaviour would have got worse and spiralled out of control if they had not had their child when they did, and believed they were now doing something much more worthwhile. Unlike many of the previous themes, this benefit is most closely correlated to the reasons provided in earlier chapters.

'I dunno – it's made me grow up – it's made me realise I can't keep being like I was ... I was just rude and obnoxious and self-centred.... It [becoming a mother] made me calm down and realise what I've gotta do now I'm not at school anymore – I'm out in the big wide world.' (female, aged 14)

'I probably would have ended up down the pan now, I expect. I would have been in a lot of – not necessarily trouble – but I would have probably been a drunk artist and on the streets drinking. It [becoming a mother] made me a lot calmer and gave me a better like, you know, a better outlook on life. I just used to drink all the time – I mean, I now only have a drink once a week.' (female, aged 17)

Despite the hard work experienced as a young parent, particularly for single mums, the majority spoke of their satisfaction with life. It was frequently accepted that it was their role now, and so it did not seem like a negative part of their lives. In fact, most young women felt that being a parent defined them now as a person and they enjoyed this new identity. This is not surprising, considering that many interviewees had a history of being surrounded by young children.

'It has been a bit ups and downs but I, I was prepared for that. Being left with a child – supporting a child – giving a, a roof over the top of the child – and also being a good mum and playing with the child and, and talking to him as well – it's hard. The bad parts, it's the screaming and – I've gotta work a way round that. But I love him and he loves me – he always comes and gives me a kiss and a cuddle when he needs it, so it's worth it all.' (female, aged 18)

'I sorta knew what it would involve and that. It never looked that hard and it's not really – everyone says I've took to it very well. I knew what to expect 'cos I've seen what it's like being a mum, and I'm not bad on no sleep.' (female, aged 18)

Improved finances and housing

Finances

Although no young women actually cited the hope of being better off as a *reason* for planning a pregnancy, many said that their financial situation had actually improved since having a baby. This was often because they were receiving state benefits, instead of relying on money from their parents or from a low-

paid job. Also, most young women considered that they had become better at managing their money since the responsibility of having a child. Often their lifestyle had drastically changed, and they were no longer spending money on themselves (for example, on clothes, alcohol and/or drugs). In some cases, young women were better off because they were now living with an employed partner. Most young women in this situation expressed surprise, and recall thinking that they would be in a much worse situation.

'Well, dramatically [better off] – I'm living on my own – well, not on my own, but without my family and (um) I'm actually claiming benefits, so I'm better off, 'cos I used to just get pocket money [laughs] before – you know. But I've – now – getting into the real world – I've got a lot of bills to pay and stuff like that.' (female, aged 18)

'I used to just cane [to spend frivolously/to waste] my money from my job on stuff for me, that I wanted – and clothes and getting drunk. I don't do that now, and I wouldn't have enough money to do that as well, even if I wanted to – which I don't, but y'know. I've got more now – I think – but I have to be more strict with it.' (female, aged 17)

Housing

Many young women reported their current local authority housing to be better than where they were living before having a child. This was particularly the case with young women who had reported bad relationships with their family, as their situation was better since living away from such a volatile environment. The housing offered by the local authority was often of a reasonable standard, and was much more appealing to the young woman than staying at home and being dependent on her family. This suggests that these young women were craving independence although, with regard to finances, it is likely that the improvement in housing acted as an effect rather than a reason for pregnancy.

'Housing-wise – in a way we're better off because we're living by ourselves, but also, when we did live – 'cos we basically lived with my mum for a while – you know – it was a house.

She was out all day, every day – so, in – but it wasn't ours, whereas this is ours. We're responsible for paying the – the rent every week [laughs] – we're responsible for putting food in the cupboard, you know.' (female, aged 16)

'Things have definitely got better. A lot better. This is like, ten – this is like, a hundred times better than it was year ago – you know – my living situation.' (female, aged 17)

Theme 2: Regret the decision to plan pregnancy

As noted before, young people regretting their pregnancy were in the minority. For those reporting a sense of regret, themes were categorised into worse finances and housing, isolation, and hard work.

Worse finances and housing

Finances

As we have seen earlier, many young women considered themselves better off financially after having a child. However, a significant proportion cited their financial situation as worse than it was before. This was mainly the case for those young women who had separated from their partners and were single mothers. In addition, some reported finding it a struggle when their partner was working because it meant they did not receive benefits anymore and had to rely solely on one wage. Finances were often cited as a major issue for these young mums, and some viewed the problem as something that might have put them off if they had known it would be so hard.

'I'm [laughs] in more debt that I was before but – (um) money – my overdraft is over the limit – I'm in big trouble with the bank for it but – no, I

still have money coming in – stuff like that. If I'd known it would be this hard, it might've made me think twice. I had more freedom before.' (female, aged 18)

'In a way, we're – we're worse off, 'cos I was working beforehand and I'm not working now – 'cos I can't get me benefits, 'cos my partner's working – we can't even get Housing Benefit and the rent here is quite expensive – so it is quite difficult, more hard than I thought probably.' (female, aged 18)

Housing

Housing quality seemed to be entirely dependent on the 'luck of the draw'. It depended on what was allocated by the local authority. This made a huge difference to how positive the young women felt about their situations in general. It was frequently reported that being allocated a run-down flat in an area with a bad reputation was something that was feared prior to allocation. For the young women who had been allocated poor housing, it was generally a constant battle to try to get out and move somewhere better. Some expressed the view that, if they had known they would be living there, it might have put them off having a child.

'At first I thought it [young mums' temporary accommodation] was all right, but now I don't like it at all, 'cos we've got three single mums living here – three – three is a crowd. I don't even think I should be here, 'cos I know that I can look after her on my own – you know what I mean – I done it in that B&B for six weeks – and even that was hard because you had one room and just a kettle and a microwave. I thought as soon as my mum wrote the letter [to say there wasn't enough room at home] I'd get somewhere on me own, but it hasn't worked out that way.' (female, aged 18)

'It's just scummy. We had damp over there, water leaking through to a huge puddle there, people drive really fast up this road, and we just found out there were squatters here before us. I don't think we should have to be here, 'cos it's not even clean. People dump stuff out there too, it's disgusting. We want to be moved. I don't want her [baby daughter] growing up thinking this is her home. They probably only gave it to us 'cos I'm young, that's what my mum thinks anyway – but my cousin got a nice place, and she's the same age.' (female, aged 18)

These different and contrasting experiences of finances and housing are most interesting. It appears that the relationship with the father of their child and the postcode 'lottery' of local authority housing allocation could dramatically change young women's personal experiences of parenthood.

Isolation

Some young women expressed regret at not being able to go out as much as they did before having a child to look after. There was a sense that their old friends had lost interest and did not include them anymore, presumably because they assumed (often correctly) they were too busy and could not afford to go out. Some young women expressed sadness about this change in their lifestyle, and wished that they could carry on as before. This loss of friendships often contributed to an isolation felt by some interviewees. For the single young mothers, it was clear that some resentment was felt that the father of their child had continued his original lifestyle. This also ties in with the fact that some interviewees felt isolated due to the housing they had been allocated.

'I wouldn't like – I wouldn't be the way like I was after it's [baby] born. 'Cos I used to – I used to drink quite a lot – I used to – I was always out but – you know – yeah – I do miss it.

I do miss it sometimes. It's hard 'cos they call me up and I can't go out like this, and that's only gonna get worse isn't it. Sometimes I feel like I should be still doing stuff like that, but I can't change it now, so....' (female, aged 17)

'I make them [friends] tell me what happened and where they've been, but I feel left out sometimes – it's not their fault – it's just, I can't go but I wish I could – or I wish I could at least see funny stuff that happened. I want them to come round all the time, but they might find her [baby daughter] boring after a while – I dunno.' (female, aged 16)

Hard work

Adding to this isolation, some young women reported struggling with the demands of new parenthood. Some, especially those lacking support from a partner or family, were finding being a mum harder and more tiring than they predicted. There was a sense of regret for rushing into becoming a young parent. Interestingly, one of these young women perceived it as very rare for people to wait until 25 years old to have a child. This illustrates that the norm for these young women is very much to have children in their late teens.

'It's not just all happy days and pink clothes and things like that, like I thought it would be – there's the sleepless nights, waking up every four hours to feed them, there is – they're very, very smelly, nappies – and there is all the worrying that goes with it. 'Cos even now I have to wake up in the middle of the night, just to make sure she's still breathing – but that's just me.' (female, aged 16)

'There's only a few very young people who say no, I'm not having a child until I'm 25 – whatever – but a lot of people do get into a relationship and speak about children – I mean, I look back and I think, I was 14 – why were we talking about marriage and children?' (female, aged 15)

Two contrasting case studies: Sarah and Becky

This section adds another dimension to understanding the reasons why young women might plan to have a child. It examines the views and experiences of two young mothers. On one hand, planning a pregnancy can be a rational choice that continues to be a positive and beneficial experience for the young woman. However, on the other hand, what was once considered to be a rational choice can turn out to be a decision that is regretted to at least some degree. These case studies help to give ideas about prevention, by showing how young women actually feel about their decisions and their lives since becoming young mothers. The first case study looks at a positive story, and the second looks at a less positive story.

Becky[3]

Background:

Becky's parents were both drug users, and she rarely attended school because she was at home looking after her younger siblings. Her father died when she was young, and she reports feeling unloved by her mother. She did not study for any GCSEs, and was not in education, employment or training when she became pregnant. She found it hard to make friends, due to not attending school. She was taking alcohol and drugs before meeting her partner.

> 'My mum and my step-dad, they're alcoholics and they're druggies as well. They do the needles and that lot. I was put in care just before my 15th birthday. He [step-dad] sexually abused me, and my mum backed him up – so, like, I don't have anything to do with any of 'em anymore. They make me sick. I always stayed at home to look after my brother and sisters, 'cos she [mother] couldn't do it – so I never had school – I never went. I went off the rails and started all of that [drinking and taking drugs], but I wised up after falling [pregnant] with E [baby daughter], 'cos I don't wanna end up like them [family].'

Planning:

Becky became pregnant when she was 17, after being with her partner for six months. They discussed becoming parents, and she became pregnant very quickly. She was not surprised, and reported feeling very happy.

> 'I haven't used any protection from the first day me and G [partner] met. I will be honest with you, (um) because we knew that we would be together for so long. We could feel it. I did a home test and it was positive, and I was really happy – and then I rang G and he was, like, over the moon.'

Reasons:

They decided to have a child together because they both loved children. They felt sure they would stay together, and wanted to be young parents to 'get it over with young', and because Becky had experienced such a disrupted home life. Becky said she wanted to have something of her own, that her parents were not involved with in any way.

> 'I always wanted children and so had G, 'cos we both got, like, bad memories of being kids so we wanted to do it right for our own. I never wanted to be one of them old mums, who can't play with her kids, and G said we should do it young and then, like, still have our lives when they've grown up. I love kids, so I knew I'd like being a mum that just stays at home.'

Reflecting:

Becky was interviewed when her child was six months old. She was still very sure that she had made the right decision in planning her pregnancy, and felt it had given her confidence and a purpose in life that she was lacking before. She was very happy, enjoyed being a mother, and accessed a range of services for young parents. Her partner is signed off work permanently due to a previous injury and mental health issues, but they have their own local authority flat and receive state benefits. Becky is currently pregnant with a second planned child.

---

3 Names have been changed.

'I wouldn't change anything, 'cos we all get on fine. She's a good baby, everyone says – and I think I'd – I'd be lost without her. And I want to be the best mum to her, and I'll go to whatever group and ask loads of questions – I don't care. I want to do the right thing and make her proud – and happy – and I'll still be young so we can be close when she's like, a teenager and stuff.'

Sarah

Background:

Sarah had a very unsettled background in an area of poverty and disadvantage, with both parents unemployed. Her mother and father separated when she was young, and her home life was quite volatile.

'My dad was there until (um) '97 and they got divorced and that was pretty bad. 'Cos he didn't wanna get divorced. My mum blackmailed him. But it was better once they'd split up, 'cos it was calmer, y'know. The fighting stopped.'

Sarah moved school a lot due to being bullied, and left before sitting her GCSEs. She frequently left home to stay with friends. She started drinking a lot, taking drugs, and was not in education, employment or training.

'We got kicked out of there and then it's been housing association, council ever since then. We've moved around loads [laughs] – I just thought it was normal, you know, trying to find a school where it [bullying] didn't happen. It just finished me off really, I didn't care about going anymore, so I didn't. And that was it – and then I didn't know what else to do and I didn't wanna work, or do nothing really. Just drinking and stuff.'

Planning:

Sarah was 16 when she became pregnant. Her partner was 18 at the time, and they had been together for six months. She reported discovering she was pregnant as a shock, despite not using contraception with her partner. The couple had decided they wanted to become parents, but they did not think it would happen so soon. Sarah reported very strong anti-abortion views.

'I was about three months when I found out so (um) I was a bit shocked – I was crying 'cos I was so shocked but, like, happy too. We didn't think it'd happen so soon, 'cos, like, you hear of people who try for ages, like, but it did. I've never believed in getting rid of a human being, 'cos that's like murder. I told my partner and he was dead happy and then we just got used to the idea – you know, I'm gonna have a baby, so everything was fine.'

Reasons:

Sarah said she wanted to escape her family and home life, and saw becoming pregnant as a way to 'grow up' and make a final break away from the family home. She also felt that she wanted to have a role, and someone to love and have responsibility for. She was hoping to give the child a stable family life, unlike her own childhood. She also loved babies, and had experience of looking after her younger brother.

'I thought it would be something just for me and J [partner], 'cos then we could just be our own family and I wouldn't be worrying about mine anymore. I wanted to just be a normal family, where the child felt loved and secure, y'know, 'cos I think that's important and I know what it's like to – y'know – not have that love and support. I've always been, like older in myself – and this didn't seem young to me, to be doing this – to be a mum.'

Reflecting:

Sarah was interviewed for this research when her child was seven months old. She said that, although she totally believed she was doing the right thing at the time, she wishes that she had waited until she was older. Her partner is now in prison and she is struggling on her own. She has not got her own local authority home and is sharing with three other young mothers. Sarah reported that she wanted a better life for her child, but it is not as she expected because she has no money or independence. She wishes she had waited until she was in a proper, secure relationship with more financial security. She also said she feels looked down on, and finds it hard to go to groups to meet other mothers.

> 'I think I rushed into it – yeah – and I thought I was in love, and I thought that person would be there for me, but they weren't. And I have to deal with that, 'cos he's [baby's father] not coming back.... I do love her [baby daughter], but I just wish – I dunno – I should've done things differently and not got, like, obsessed by wanting one – y'know, 'cos I thought it would make me happy – and it has – but not what I thought. It's hard, I've got no money, and I need somewhere for just me and her – and I get down – I'm having counselling and stuff. I see other families and I think 'that's what I wanted for me', but it didn't happen like that.'

Summary of chapter findings

It is, once again, clear from this chapter that young mothers are far from an homogeneous group who all view being a parent in the same way. Most of the young women were pleased with their decision to become a parent. Many reported numerous benefits of their new life, with some of these benefits being unexpected. This serves only to justify what has been, for the majority of this sample, a highly rational decision. However, in contrast, several openly regretted their decision to plan their pregnancy. From a practice point of view, sharing these views with other teenagers could provide an valuable insight into such an important decision. The two main themes, with sub-themes, are summarised below:

Pleased with the decision to plan pregnancy

1. Happiness and fulfilment:
   The majority of interviewees reported feeling happier now, compared with before becoming pregnant. This was due to feeling more fulfilled, having a new purpose and role, and becoming more confident. It was also common for interviewees to say that they would be in a worse situation if they had not had their child. Other benefits were feeling closer to their family.
2. Improved finances and housing:
   More interviewees than expected reported having more money and living in better accommodation since becoming a parent. Often this was due to leaving the family home, becoming independent, and learning to manage money better. Some interviewees reported being surprised at this improvement, because they were not expecting it, indicating that it was not a motivating factor.

Regret the decision to plan pregnancy

1. Worse finances and housing:
   Despite many young women saying they felt better off, a significant number of interviewees felt worse off in these areas of their lives. This seemed to be governed by their relationship situation, and where they moved to as a result of living away from their family.

2. Isolation:

   Some interviewees reported feeling isolated from their friends, due to having a child. This was reported by young single mothers more, and resentment was often displayed at the fact that the father of the child could still have a good social life. These feelings of isolation were exacerbated by being placed in accommodation they did not like.

3. Hard work:

   Some young women were surprised and often overwhelmed by the strain and hard work of bringing up a child. Again, this was worse among those who were raising their child as a single parent.

As a final note, despite the fact that these young women were experiencing poverty and disadvantage, they were mainly positive about their decision to plan their pregnancy. Reflecting as new parents, the majority of young women felt that they had made the right decision and that things had turned out more favourably than they had imagined. The extent to which these positive reflections will be sustained is still open to question (as most women interviewed had a child less than one year old). These positive accounts, however, do not diminish the importance of those who had regrets, and there are learning points here regarding prevention and education. Also, it is possible the regrets were under-reported by some young women, for fear of insinuating that their child was unwanted.

Young fathers

7

This chapter is dedicated entirely to exploring the views and experiences of young fathers. It examines the findings from the 10 one-to-one interviews with young fathers facing poverty and disadvantage, who 'planned' to have a child with their partner. Although only 10 fathers were interviewed, this part of the research adds another important dimension to the findings. As far as we are aware, no other research has explored the views of young fathers in this context. Before presenting the findings, it is worth noting the difficulties of recruiting this sub-sample. Unlike the young mothers, the fathers were rarely attending any parenting support groups. As a consequence, an alternative means of recruitment was used. Most of the young fathers who were interviewed were recruited from groups that had taken referrals from Youth Offending Teams (YOTs). Although all were facing poverty and disadvantage, this process of recruitment needs to be recognised when interpreting the findings (that is, compared with other young fathers in the sample, these young men may have more complex lives and experiences which have led to their motivations for planning).

This chapter opens by giving a profile of the interviewees. It goes on to discuss how the young fathers' reasons for planning a child differed from those of the young mothers. The two groups shared some reasons, however, and these will also be briefly discussed. Nevertheless, it is thought that the interest lies in examining the *different* motivating factors between the young mothers and young fathers. It should also be considered that, generally, men do not 'open up' as much as women in the interview situation. This could be due to a number of reasons, for example, male

interviewees thinking it is inappropriate for a man to talk about his feelings on this subject, and/or embarrassment in front of a female interviewer.

Recruitment and interviewee profile

As with the young mothers in this research, the London Measure of Unplanned Pregnancy or LMUP (Barrett et al, 2004) was integral in ensuring that we interviewed only those who had planned to become a parent. However, it was essential to change the wording of some questions for its use with young fathers (such as 'did your partner…'). The young father's questionnaire is attached in Appendix B. This adapted version, however, has not been validated. The average score on the questionnaire was 10 out of 14 (14 being the highest possible score), indicating a fairly high level of planning. One half of the 50 questionnaires sent to young fathers' groups (primarily via YOTs) were returned. As with the young mothers, the researcher followed up the eligible young fathers and arranged interviews.

Age

Of the 10 young fathers interviewed, two measures of age were recorded: age at first planned pregnancy (Figure 6), and age at interview (Figure 7). The discrepancy in age profiles reflects the fact that, in some cases, some time had elapsed between their partner's pregnancy and the interview.

Figure 6: Age of young fathers at first 'planned' pregnancy

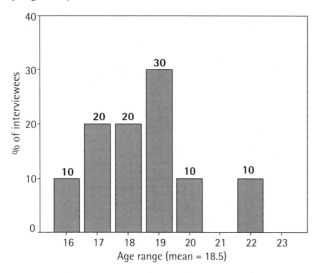

Figure 7: Age of young fathers at interview

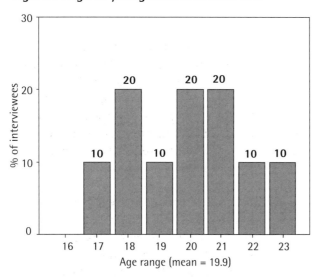

Parental status

Of the interviewees, the vast majority (nine out of 10 young fathers) were now parents. The partner of the remaining interviewee was expecting their first planned child. Three interviewees had other children, the majority of which had been planned.

Geographical spread

The range of geographical locations is not as wide for the young fathers as for the young mothers, mainly due to the small number of interviewees. Questionnaires were distributed to young fathers' groups in a variety of locations in England, but it proved challenging to find young fathers' to interview. This was mainly because many fathers' groups were just beginning, and had not built up a client base yet. Also, some young fathers did not volunteer for interview on their LMUP. Therefore, the majority of interviewees were local to the research centre (six out of 10 from East Sussex), with a further two from Durham and two from Yorkshire.

Poverty and disadvantage

All interviewees experienced poverty and disadvantage, similar to the experiences of the young mothers outlined in Chapter 2. Material disadvantage during childhood and in the year prior to their partner becoming pregnant was evident.

Reasons for planning: reasons in common with young mothers

Although not always as detailed, the young fathers gave many reasons for planning that were very similar to those given by the young women who had been interviewed. This shows a degree of consistency in the findings irrespective of gender. This is likely to be due to the fact that all interviewees were from similar levels of poverty and disadvantage, and thus many of their experiences and factors leading them to make this life-choice were similar. The main similarities are detailed below:

Unsettled and turbulent background

All of the young fathers had experienced a turbulent childhood. It was very common to be in a one-parent family, and levels of poverty and disadvantage were relatively high. Most young men reported mainly bad memories, and this was mostly due to feeling unsettled, unwanted, and experiencing negative relationships with other family members.

> 'I don't know – it was crap, really. I've got all bad memories, looking back. It was just me and my mum, and she wasn't that interested – well, she was, but she wasn't – she didn't show it.'

She's one of them – not maternal, if you know ...' (male, aged 16[4])

'It was hard, really – we didn't have much and we could never afford to do anything, and my mum always felt guilty – like, 'cos she couldn't get us stuff – it weren't her fault but she thought she should be – y'know – getting stuff for us. But we were ok, just poor I guess! [laughs]' (male, aged 18)

A very small number of interviewees mentioned that these factors had been influential in their decision to have a child, but generally this was just accepted, and not viewed as a reason for becoming a young father.

Negative experiences at school

All the young fathers who were interviewed had experienced problems at school. These ranged from truanting and not sitting GCSEs, to being excluded. Reasons for these problems at school included bullying, but were mainly around extreme disinterest and boredom. Due to a lack of qualifications, interviewees found it hard to get into college or get a job. Those who did find employment were mainly in short-term, manual work. Some young men did not work. A small minority did not want to and did not plan to, but most were seeking employment although finding it hard to secure a job.

'I hated school, I didn't see the point. It was all 'do this, do that', and I couldn't stand it. I hated it, and I hated the teachers. It bored me, so that's why I caused trouble – something to do innit. [laughs].' (male, aged 17)

'I was meant to be starting a bricky job but I only went for two days, and the – I dunno – I didn't really like it so I didn't carry it on. I'm gonna do something – I just don't know what yet, I'm thinking about it. [laughs]' (male, aged 18)

The fact that *all* young fathers had had some degree of problems at school could indicate that such young men are more 'at risk' of becoming a young parent. It could be that they focus on other aspects of their lives, for example, by becoming a parent, to give them a purpose other than academia and/or employment.

'I left school, and then I met S [baby's mother] and that went really well – it was good, and I know we were young but I felt ready. I was, like, always too old for school, well – I felt like that.' (male, aged 18)

Social and family norms in the local area

Most young men reported that young parenthood was not unusual in their area. This shows that teenage parenthood could be perpetuated in areas, by becoming the 'norm'. Some interviewees expressed surprise that we were interested in conducting research into young fatherhood, because it was so common where they lived.

'Most people I know, they got a kid. It's not like I'm the only one my age – it's fine. It's normal. My mum was the one asking when we was gonna have one, but I was like 'Whoa, wait a bit!', but then we had her [baby daughter]. But, round here, it's not young – I don't think it's young, neither.' (male, aged 18)

A love of babies, and experience of caring for them

Some young men said that they had always wanted to be a father because there were a lot of babies in their family and they were used to looking after them. Some young men also reported that they had always loved spending time with babies and young children.

'I've always loved little 'uns – they're wicked. I get on with them, and they always come to me, my nieces. I love 'em, and I don't see why that should

---

4   As before, age refers to age at first planned conception.

be weird – like, for a man to like babies. I get on with kids better than adults. [laughs] I always have.' (male, aged 16)

Reasons for planning: reasons unique to young fathers

Arguably of more interest are the reasons for planning that were unique to the young fathers' interviews. This allows us to achieve a useful comparison between the sexes, and get a real insight into the situation a young man is in, in the planning dynamic. We can see that some motivating factors are, in fact, unique to being male.

Planning

Perhaps unsurprisingly, planning varied drastically between the perspectives of the young mothers and the young fathers. Although the majority of the young fathers interviewed said that their child was planned, it was always their partner who had taken the lead with this. For instance it was generally the partner who had *suggested* 'trying' for a baby, and who had persuaded the young man that having a child together was a good idea. From there, the interviewees reported being excited and wanting to become a father. This is interesting, because not one of the young fathers reported being the one who suggested having a child. This idea that women have the more powerful role to play in planning suggests that prevention could focus on young men, and how they could potentially be more assertive in the decision to plan a pregnancy.

'She [mother of child] just said 'why don't we have one?', and then at first I thought 'nah, it's too soon', but then I thought it'd be quite good, and I thought it wouldn't happen for ages anyway, 'cos most people – like, try for ages don't they? But, it was like, two months and she was like 'I'm pregnant', which was cool, 'cos by then I wanted to – I like, really wanted to be a dad by then.' (male, aged 18)

'L [mother of child] said we should, like, try for one because we'd been together for a while and she wanted one, and we'd been having problems and she thought it'd bring us – like, y'know – back closer. Then I started thinking it'd be good, especially if it was a boy and then I could, like, play with it.' (male, aged 17)

Lack of a father figure

Notably, only one out of the 10 young fathers interviewed had grown up with a steady father figure in the home. The other nine young fathers either had no father figure, a series of different ones, or they had been in care.

'I never saw my dad. He came in and out, like, but we never spoke and I hated him. We argued – didn't get on. I didn't like how he was with my mum, then he left. I think of myself like, I – like I didn't have a dad really. It was always just us and that was hard but, now I think we were better off without him really.' (male, aged 18)

In many cases, the interviewees reported that this was influential in the decision to become a young father. This was usually because they wanted to prove that they could do a better job of being a father, because they had experienced a childhood without a father. This was one of the few reasons provided by young fathers that was explicitly linked towards their planning a pregnancy.

'I think I wanted to be a parent young, y'know, so I could be a good dad. I didn't have a dad, so I wanted to see if I could do it, and give him [baby son] more than what I had really. I don't know if that's much of a reason, but how – it's what I always thought really – and luckily it happened, really quickly for us.' (male, aged 19)

'My dad left before I was born, but I see him now – we only met, like, a year ago. I see him every week – he sees E [baby daughter] and stuff sometimes – I'm still getting to know him really. I, like [laughs] – I'd started to think he didn't exist, and then I found him. I think he found it too hard, 'cos he was only young himself when my mum had me, and he couldn't handle it – so he left. Dunno, I know what's it's like to wonder all the time, and I couldn't do that – to E.' (male, aged 18)

Criminal background

As noted at the beginning of this chapter, some interviewees had been referred by a YOT to the young fathers' group they were attending. Five out of the 10 young fathers had spent time in a young offenders institution. For four of these young men, becoming a father had happened within a year of coming out and, for the remaining one, it had happened just before he went in. It is hard to make generalisations from this small number of fathers. Nonetheless, it is interesting to consider whether planning to become a young father was connected to a background of being in trouble, and spending time in a young offenders institution.

'It's the way I am, I'm quite old for my age. It's like, I got all my, like aggression out of my system when I was younger, and so now I'm – more – more, y'know – more mature so I was ready to have a kid. I'm not like other 18-year-olds, 'cos I done all that stuff and I'm bored of it now. All my mates are in their twenties and thirties – I can't stand to be around people my own age who are still messing about. I know where it's gonna get 'em.' (male, aged 18)

'I've always done what I wanted really. It's my fault I ended up in trouble, and in there. And it's my fault I've got a kid now. I've always done stuff I'm not supposed to – it's just me. If I see it and I want it, I just decide I'm gonna have it, and that's like – that's like the story of my life – and I don't know why. [laughs] I don't think about what could happen.' (male, aged 17)

It was also interesting to note that the new responsibility of having a child made the young fathers say that they wanted to stay out of trouble. In this way, it seems that having a child was a settling influence.

'I spent a year in there, but when I got out I met L [mother of child] and she fell pregnant within about three months. So, I can't risk going back now, 'cos I've got a family, and someone else to think about.' (male, aged 19)

'I was in there when he [baby son] was born, and it killed me. It made me realise that I can't do it again – I'm not gonna get in that situation again. I don't think they should put you away if you've got a kiddie on the way – it's not fair on them, is it?' (male, aged aged 20)

Not sure of reasons

It is worth noting here that some male interviewees did not seem to be sure about their reasons for planning to become a parent. This was typical of a lot of the interviewees' accounts, and was probably the leading difference between the young women's and men's accounts. This is interesting because, if young fathers themselves do not know their motivations for planning a child, it is very hard to design interventions in response. It could be that the young men had never really considered their motivations. It seemed to be something that 'just happened'.

'I don't know – maybe not having a dad around made me – like, I don't know – want a son or something. But I don't know – it could have, but I think I maybe would've, like, wanted one anyway.' (male, aged 17)

'I don't know, there wasn't a reason really. We just talked about it, she wanted one, and then we had one. It was simple really. I couldn't tell you why. It just happened, and it was good, but it wasn't like, anything deep.' (male, aged 16)

'I don't know what my reasons were. I didn't have any really. It just seemed like a good idea, and I knew she [baby's mother] wanted one, so I just went along with it really. It was fine.' (male, aged 18)

Reflecting

In general, the positive aspects highlighted by young fathers were similar to those given by young women, such as having a new 'direction'. Overall, the young fathers interviewed were more likely to express regret at their decision, compared with young mothers. Regret was mostly expressed in terms of not seeing their child. If the couple separated, the young father was the one who was often excluded from the child's life. Feelings of bitterness were common in the interviews with young fathers, which often led to feeling regret at becoming a father in the first place. This could be something to focus on in interventions aimed at young fathers (in other words, the fact that having a child is a big decision, because parental separation can easily occur).

'Well, I never – I'm not allowed to see J [baby son] anymore, so in a way I wish I never had got involved with her [baby's mother]. It's been nothing but trouble and now I wish I'd had one with someone I was gonna stay with. I want J, but the father always gets the worse deal, doesn't he?' (male, aged 18)

'I think she [baby's mother] used me to get a baby, and now I'm not allowed to see D [baby son]. She was all like 'I want to have a baby with you', but I think she just wanted to get one to get a flat and then I wasn't any use to her, and I was out of the picture. It pisses me off, but I can't do anything.' (male, aged 19)

Summary of chapter findings

Although the number of young fathers interviewed is small, their views and experiences are interesting. Their accounts of planning, and their reasons for wanting a child, were often different from those of the young mothers, and thus they provide some

interesting insights into the role of the male in planning.

Interestingly, although many parents generally worry about not being able to provide for their children, this was not a main concern of these young fathers. They were more concerned about not being there for their children. This was perhaps because they themselves were not used to having lots of material things. However, they were used to a lack of love and, more specifically, the lack of a father. Despite the fact that the majority of interviewees were not employed, and they were living in local authority accommodation, money worries were not frequently cited.

Some young fathers seemed to genuinely not know their reasons for wanting a child, and some were heavily influenced by their partner and did not seem to be very active in the actual planning stage. It seems that some young men are vulnerable to becoming young fathers: when they are not totally sure about it; because of their partner's wish to have a child; and the fact that the woman, as biology dictates, is in a more powerful position to decide this. The interviewees had many background factors in common, and so this chapter highlights potential ideas for interventions to perhaps identify vulnerable young men, and maybe look at ways to deter them from the idea of young parenthood. Of greatest interest is the young men's lack of a positive male role model in their lives, their lack of involvement in instigating a discussion around planning a child, and other factors that might make a young man more 'at risk' of becoming a young father (such as having been 'off the rails' and in trouble with the law). Interventions could be designed around young men's opinions on these matters, and at the same time focusing on negotiation, confidence-building, and encouraging more young men into education, training or employment. This is especially relevant considering the high proportion of the sample who are not in education, employment or training.

Reasons for planning: reasons in common with young mothers

1. Unsettled and turbulent background:
   The interviewees shared many characteristics, such as an unsettled and turbulent background relating to negative family relationships.
2. Negative experiences at school:
   All interviewees left school without sitting their GCSEs, either due to truanting and leaving, or being excluded. All have struggled to settle to any employment or training since.
3. Social and family norms in the local area:
   Some young men expressed surprise that they were the topic of research, because young parenthood was so prominent in their area. It is likely that this is due to the specific areas selected for this research.
4. A love of babies, and experience of caring for them:
   Some young men reported always wanting to be a father, and enjoying spending time with and looking after babies. This was a key motivating factor.

Reasons for planning: reasons unique to young fathers

1. Planning:
   Some young men were not very active in the planning stage, and reported agreeing to have a baby at their partner's suggestion. The young men then got used to the idea and started wanting a child. It seems that their partners had a big persuasive influence.
2. Lack of a father figure:
   The vast majority of interviewees did not have a steady father figure when they were growing up, and most interviewees said that this had affected their decision. They wanted to be a better father. This was the reason that was most explicitly linked to planning a pregnancy.
3. Criminal background:
   Five out of 10 interviewees had been referred to the recruitment site through a YOT. Some cited their experiences with crime as influential in their decision to become a young father, and as important in making them want to stay out of trouble for their child.

4. 'Not sure' of reasons:
   Interestingly, many young fathers could not answer questions relating to why they wanted to become a young father. This could be due to communication issues, or perhaps they had never thought about this specifically before.
5. Reflecting:
   A greater proportion of young fathers regretted their decision to become a parent compared with young mothers. Some fathers were upset because they had split up from their partner and were not allowed to spend time with their children. Some interviewees felt they had been used by their ex-partner so that she could have a child.

8

Conclusions and implications

Introduction

This study exploring the motivations for young people's 'planned' pregnancies has generated a number of findings that will be of relevance to researchers, policy makers and practitioners.

Beforehand, it is important to place the findings from this study into their correct context. It is essential to appreciate that this study of 41 young mothers (or mothers-to-be) and 10 young fathers is not claimed to be statistically representative of all young parents, and that all participants were of White British ethnicity. Because this study was conducted in England, caution should be applied when extending the findings and implications to other countries. This is due to different teenage pregnancy rates and policy contexts.

Although recruited from a range of locations throughout England, the sample is skewed in two ways. First, only young people who had, or were experiencing poverty and disadvantage were included in the study. Poverty and disadvantage was defined in its widest form, including financial, geographical, material and emotional hardship. Planned pregnancies among young people who had not experienced poverty and disadvantage were not included in this study (and obviously this is an area in need of more research). Second, only those young people who volunteered for interview were included. In light of discussions with key workers, it is apparent that the younger parents (especially the 15- and 16-year-olds) were far less likely to volunteer, and thus may be underrepresented in this sample. Nonetheless, in such a qualitative and relatively small-scale study, these features of the sample are offset by the extremely rich and detailed

insight that these 51 young people have provided.

Having placed the study into context, in terms of its underlying methodology, this final chapter also includes a brief summary of the main themes and explanations derived from the interviews:

- All young women interviewed experienced poverty and disadvantage during their childhood (over two thirds of the sample were living in the upper quarter of deprived wards in England). **Chapter 2**
- All the young women interviewed reported having planned their pregnancy. This ranged from people discussing this openly with partners and taking steps to ensure a positive and healthy pregnancy, to those who were more fatalistic about the prospects of pregnancy (that is, stopped the use of contraception, or used contraception inconsistently). All interviewees were aware of how to use contraception, although some did not connect lack of contraception with the real possibility of becoming pregnant, often taking a more fatalistic view. **Chapter 3**
- Although planned, the majority of young women kept this secret from their family in the first instance. Many reported 'shock' and were adamant that terminating the pregnancy was not an option. **Chapter 3**
- The majority of the reasons were not child-specific (for example, love for a child or 'a natural stage in our relationship'). In contrast, reasons were more related to the current situation young people were in. **Chapters 3-7**
- Childhood and background factors, although not always explicitly stated, were

instrumental in the young women's decisions to become pregnant. An unsettled background (for example, a difficult and often traumatic family upbringing) and negative experiences at school, resulting in poor educational attainment, provided an impetus to 'change direction' in their life. **Chapter 4**

- The local geography or area impacted on decisions to choose pregnancy. This was a product of limited employment or training opportunities, poor and expensive transport costs in rural areas, and the high visibility and acceptance of other young parents in the neighbourhood. **Chapters 4 and 5**

- Choosing to become pregnant was seen as an opportunity, one that was within their own control, to change their life for the better. Becoming a parent was a route out of family hardship and unhappiness, a chance for independence, and an opportunity to gain a new identity. **Chapter 5**

- Parenthood provided an opportunity to create a loving family of one's own and, in a sense, to compensate for their own negative childhood experiences. Bringing up a baby was perceived as providing a purpose, one that provided a sense of capability and satisfaction, and was better than having a low-paid, 'dead-end' job. **Chapter 5**

- Many young women reported reasons for planning their pregnancy that are generic for most parents. Many spoke of the love of babies, often heightened by experiences of caring for babies throughout their early life. Also, several viewed 'getting it out of the way' as a motivation, which would enable them to have a good and 'youthful' relationship with their child in the future, while still being young enough to enjoy their own life. **Chapter 5**

- The majority of the sample reported the pleasures of parenthood, which affirmed their seemingly rational decision. In reflecting on their life before pregnancy, most reported how their life had improved, as they had hoped it would. Many said that their life would have been far worse if they had not become a parent – through continued family disruption and unhappiness, the growing sense of worthlessness and lack of direction and, for some, worsening alcohol and drug use. **Chapter 6**

- Many of the improvements that young parenthood brought were unexpected, but viewed as a positive. They were not foreseen at the time of becoming pregnant and, in this sense, provided even more justification that this decision had been the right one. These positives included unexpected improvements in housing and finances, increased confidence and fulfilment, and closer family relationships. Contrary to some public opinion, improved housing was rarely reported as a motivation for pregnancy. **Chapter 6**

- For a minority, however, pregnancy and parenthood had not fulfilled their expectations. These women reported their lives had worsened due to increased financial worries, poor housing, a sense of isolation from friends and other people their own age, and the sheer hard work and demands. These concerns were more prevalent among 'single mothers' who lacked support. **Chapter 6**

- With the exception of the minority who regretted their pregnancy, the findings from this study illustrate the seemingly rational and positive decision of choosing the new lifecourse of parenthood. This clearly challenges the stereotypical viewpoint of teenage pregnancy as a solely negative life-choice. It could be that, in some situations, having a baby can represent a rational decision with some beneficial outcomes. **Chapters 3-7**

- Regarding young fathers, some reasons for planning a child were similar to reasons young mothers gave. For example, reasons relating to the experience of an unhappy and unsettled childhood, negative experiences at school, liking babies and having experience of looking after them, and being aware that young parenthood was prominent in their local area. **Chapter 7**

- Other reasons given by young fathers were very different, and unique to their accounts. For example, reasons relating to a lack of a father figure, the impact of having a criminal background and wanting to be there for their child, and their different input in the planning stage (in other words, notably less than the mother). Young fathers interviewed were also more likely than mothers to regret their decision to become a parent. **Chapter 7**

In light of these main findings, the implications from this research will be presented in two parts:

- Implications for research
- Implications for policy and practice

Implications for research

As outlined in Chapter 1, the concept of planned pregnancy in young people has rarely been explored in research. Where decisions in relation to pregnancy have been explored, most studies have focused on post-conception decisionmaking. As such, studies by Tabberer et al (2000), Lee et al (2004) and Turner (2004) have explored young women's decisions regarding pregnancy termination. Although assumed to be mainly unplanned pregnancies, these studies have provided some findings that correlate with this research. For example, young people who recognised the visibility of young motherhood in their local area were found to be more 'pro-life' and likely to choose to continue with their pregnancy (Tabberer et al, 2000).

This acceptance within the local neighbourhood clearly ties in with the 'social and family norms in the local area' finding outlined in Chapter 4. Lee et al (2004) also found evidence of this local acceptance, and extended this understanding by recognising that young women from disadvantaged and insecure backgrounds were more likely to see parenthood as a positive change. Indeed, Arai (2003) argues that as a means of escaping adversity, youthful parenthood should be recognised as a mature and meaningful option. Perceiving parenthood as a positive, alternative lifecourse is central to the 'childhood unsettlement' outlined in Chapter 4 and the 'needs' expressed in Chapter 5. Similarly, Turner's 'acceptance' theory (2004) argues that young people who have lower expectations are more likely to predict that, if pregnant, they would continue the pregnancy to full term. Low expectations and few perceived opportunities for education, employment, or alternative direction in life were, again, central themes to the experiences of the young people interviewed in this study. This was evident in young women's negative experiences in school (Chapter 4), and the 'gaining a purpose to their life' theme outlined in Chapter 5. Many of these themes were relevant to young men as well (Chapter 7). Furthermore, the fact that many of these explanations relate to adversity and low expectations, it becomes easier to understand the link between poverty, disadvantage and teenage pregnancy (Botting et al, 1998; Dennison, 2004).

From the review of the literature outlined in Chapter 1, we were only able to identify two US-based studies that specifically looked at the decisions and motivations for planned pregnancy among young people. These studies are clearly the closest, in terms of research evidence, to the study outlined in this report. Murray (1990) was one of the first to openly argue that most teenage pregnancies are planned in order to gain access to local authority housing. In contrast to this argument, our research would suggest that most teenage parents are not aware of this and other entitlements until they become pregnant (Allen and Bourke-Dowling, 1998; YWCA, 2005). The most notable study into 'planned adolescent pregnancy' was conducted by Montgomery (2002) among a small sample of eight young women who became pregnant intentionally. There are several conclusions from Montgomery's work that are parallel to those reported here. The desire for an alternative lifecourse, due to childhood adversity or limited life-options, clearly ties in with Montgomery's 'needs' for pregnancy. Of their reported needs it is clear that the desire for stability and settlement reported by our sample is more significant as a motivation than Montgomery's 'financial need'. In fact, the financial implications in our study were rarely considered before pregnancy, and also worked both ways in terms of having positive and negative implications. The desire for independence, love of a child, and wanting to feel more grown-up also tie in with Montgomery's 'wants' for pregnancy. In slight contrast, however, the 'want' for a child as a natural step in a relationship was, interestingly, rarely mentioned in our research although may have been implicit throughout. All this considered, it is quite clear that our study will make a valuable contribution to the limited existing research in this area.

A key conclusion to draw from this study is that planned pregnancies, among people as young as 13 years of age, do exist in this country. This evidence supports those studies that also report planned pregnancies among teenagers (Kiernan, 1995; BMRB, 2001, 2003; Barrett et al, 2004; MacDonald and Marsh, 2005), and provides the richest data to date by using a one-to-one, qualitative approach.

Implications for policy and practice

The policy context in England surrounding teenage pregnancy is oriented towards the prevention of unintended pregnancy, which is due in part to the lack of knowledge and evidence regarding the existence and reasons for planned pregnancy. Given that around one third of all teenage pregnancies result in a termination (ONS, 2005), it is clear that a sizeable proportion of these conceptions were initially unintended. However, this research has reported evidence of planned pregnancies and has highlighted the often rational, conscious decisions at work. Of the two thirds of conceptions that do result in childbirth, it is simply not possible to know the proportion that was originally planned or unplanned.

This research casts some doubt on the argument posited in the Teenage Pregnancy Strategy that, 'in practice, the first conscious decision that many teenagers make about their pregnancy is whether to have an abortion or to continue with the pregnancy' (SEU, 1999, p 28). For the teenagers in this research, it appears that decisions around pregnancy occurred prior to conception. In view of this and other policies, it is reasonable to conclude that the issue of intended or planned teenage pregnancy has not received sufficient attention or recognition. This research provides a starting point for young people's issues and experiences around planned teenage pregnancy to be heard.

At the very least, the experiences of those young women and men who plan their pregnancies as teenagers need to be shared with practitioners working closely with such groups. These practitioners will include youth workers, Connexions personal advisers, teachers and social workers who all work with young people before conception, as well as teenage pregnancy coordinators, teenage–parent support workers, midwives and health

visiters who work closely with young parents or single mothers who are pregnant. Understanding the primary motivations for becoming pregnant as teenagers will be of great interest to such professionals. The importance of childhood and background disadvantage, and how this impacts on young people's decisions regarding pregnancy will be of particular use. Acknowledging the leading motivations behind pregnancy, and sharing these with young people, could help to enable better-informed decisions around pregnancy.

In view of implications for policy and practice, there are two elements of the research that will be outlined. First, we shall detail areas of specific concern that have been drawn out from this research. Second, we shall present a non-partisan viewpoint over whether teenage pregnancy, when planned, should be viewed as a 'problem' for today's society.

Specific issues for concern

There are four areas of concern drawn from this research that will be of interest to policy makers and practitioners.

1. Different types of planning:
   As noted in Chapters 2 and 3, there is much complexity over how young people define planning in relation to pregnancy. This may help to explain why some young people define their pregnancies as 'unplanned' although also stating that they were not using contraception. Planning is rarely comprehended dichotomously, with young people reporting different extents to which their pregnancy was planned. For some young people, particularly those classified as 'definitely planned', the decision to become pregnant was made with careful consideration and involvement of the partner. However, in some cases, and of greater concern, pregnancies were planned with minimal involvement of the partner. As shown in Chapter 3, some pregnancies arose from scenarios where the partner was not at all involved in the planning. In these cases, unsurprisingly, it was mostly the women who took this decision with the young men being unaware of their intentions. In reality, control was taken by the young women in stopping their use of the contraceptive Pill,

without disclosing this to their partner. Although not covered in this research, it could be assumed that a pregnancy arising without the male partner's consent could prove to be more detrimental to the future of the parental relationship, and ultimately to the well-being of the child. Pregnancies arising in these instances also have implications for the young men who are not always in control of the situation if contraception is reliant on the Pill. Young men would clearly be able to have more say in the outcome if condoms were used. The views of the young fathers illustrate in more detail how the women had more say in the outcome.

2. Information needs:
In the analysis of young women's discussions of planning and first reactions to pregnancy, there were evident concerns about young people's factual knowledge around pregnancy. For some young people, stopping the use of contraception was not always connected to the potential for pregnancy. By contrast, stopping the use of contraception, or in reality using contraception inconsistently, would render the prospect of pregnancy to the 'lap of the gods'. There were numerous occasions in this research where young people spoke of 'falling pregnant', 'if it happens it happens' and 'that's up to my body'. This is most interesting as all were aware of the purpose of contraception, but still did not fully recognise the possibility of pregnancy if it was no longer used. Given these findings, there is a clear need to inform young people that they have the ultimate control over whether they become pregnant. Consequently, they can have the certainty of avoiding pregnancy if they use contraception. Similarly, there is a need to inform young people that there is a potential for immediate pregnancy if contraception is not used. It seems that there is also a need to include 'fertility' in sex and relationships education, in order to illustrate to young people just how fertile they are in their teenage years because some were unaware and even worried about infertility.

3. Support needs:
As alluded to earlier, a key worker is likely to be in contact with a number of young people reporting different degrees of pregnancy planning. In acknowledging that young people report pregnancy and arrive as parents through different processes (from complete 'accidents' to 'definitely planned'), there may well be different support needs. For example, those pregnant resulting from 'accidents' or unintentionally may be more overwhelmed at the outset and require more support with either decisions around termination, or throughout their pregnancy and early experiences of parenthood. In contrast, those who planned their pregnancy may in some sense have a 'head-start' in preparing for parenthood, in that the potential for pregnancy has been considered prior to conception. Nonetheless, for some young people becoming pregnant intentionally, the realities and responsibilities of parenthood may need to be emphasised as their expectations of being parents may prove unrealistic. There are also opportunities for linking in relationship and parenting skills before, during and following pregnancy.

In addition, for those planning a pregnancy following a miscarriage it is possible that some young women intend to become pregnant again for fear that having a miscarriage means they may not be able to become parents in the future. Clearly more follow-up and counselling after such an event could enable young people to make a more informed choice about future pregnancies.

4. Regrets:
Although most people report rational and fully justified reasons for pregnancy, learning the lessons from those whose expectations were not met has an important role to play. The experiences of those openly regretting pregnancy is important information that should be shared with teenagers considering such a lifecourse. Young people who have since regretted their pregnancy is arguably the greatest concern to arise from this research. In conjunction with the findings outlined in Chapter 6, the possibility of worse finances and housing, and the likely hard and demanding work involved in becoming a parent need to be acknowledged. In addition, the sense of isolation and distancing from friendship and support groups as a potential outcome needs to be recognised. In almost all instances, these regretted outcomes are exacerbated among 'single mothers', and

may therefore tie in with the findings relating to partner involvement in decision making. Without intending to paint an overly negative picture of teenage pregnancy, these accounts of those young people who found pregnancy to be more difficult than expected are a real contribution of this research. Sharing these outcomes with young people considering pregnancy, possibly through peer education, may help this decision to become as well informed as possible. Focusing efforts on those most likely to become teenage parents could be an efficient approach. From the young fathers who were interviewed, it would appear that these messages should be conveyed to young men in particular, perhaps in comprehensive sex and relationships education. For those young fathers who reported regrets, these were centred around not being able to have contact with the child following parental separation.

An objective view of planned teenage pregnancy

It is important to state at the outset that the authors of this report do not support any particular view or standpoint as to whether planned teenage pregnancy should be perceived as a problem for today's society. By contrast, in recognising that planned teenage pregnancy does exist, we hope this research will enable readers to appreciate two contrasting perspectives. These contrasting perspectives will be outlined in turn.

1. Preventing teenage pregnancy:
   In consideration of the motivations for planned teenage pregnancy, there are clear implications for prevention. The majority of young people's motivations were driven from their experiences of poverty and disadvantage. For most, pregnancy was seen as a means to change their lifecourse for the better, by escaping family problems, erasing the memories of a hard and unsettled upbringing and a desire for independence. Rarely was pregnancy viewed as a 'natural step in the relationship', or a life-choice that felt 'right at this present time'.

   It is clear from the young people's motivations that poverty and disadvantage

connect closely to teenage pregnancy, and especially those pregnancies that are planned. That is, poverty and disadvantage in its widest sense: from financial hardship through to emotional disadvantage. Although lessons can be learned from this research to prevent teenage pregnancy, the social and economic divide in this country is unequivocally linked to youthful parenthood. The obvious parallel is the social divide in the US where teenage pregnancy rates are higher than in England, in stark contrast to more egalitarian societies in Western Europe which have lower teenage pregnancy rates than England (SEU, 1999). For as long as this social divide is maintained, mirrored in terms of opportunities for education, training and employment, the desire to choose pregnancy as an alternative lifecourse among those facing poverty and disadvantage will be maintained.

The desire for an alternative direction in life offers clear potential for the prevention of teenage pregnancy. It was evident that pregnancy was perceived as a lifecourse that young people, especially young women, had total control over. In relation to pregnancy prevention, the question arises as to alternative means of changing direction. At this point, it is clear through the young people's accounts that training and employment opportunities were rare. Making education, training and employment opportunities accessible to young people could provide an alternative lifecourse to pregnancy. These opportunities could provide independence and a potential to change direction, in an alternative way. Numerous accounts of poor educational experiences and 'dead-end jobs' support this important point.

Although much is being done to provide these opportunities for young parents (SEU, 1999), it is notable from this research that these opportunities need to be focused on young people at an earlier stage in their life. One possibility could be to offer opportunities for young people to explore the various options available to them at different stages in their lives. Working with young people in this manner, before they can conceive, and perhaps focusing on those groups who are most likely to plan their pregnancies could be a way forward (based on the contributing factors outlined in this report). Ultimately, this could maintain young people's interest and raise their expectations surrounding education, employment and alternative opportunities in life besides youthful parenthood. Of these alternatives, it appears that educational experiences and attainment are most central to these pregnancy decisions, arguably beyond the poor and deprived upbringings.

2. Why prevent teenage pregnancy?
Given that most people in this study reported rational reasons for becoming pregnant, and that the vast majority stated that their lives have since improved in many ways, the necessity to prevent planned teenage pregnancy must be open to debate. For the young people in this study, becoming pregnant had provided them with a means to improve their lives, by becoming independent, giving them a sense of purpose, escaping poor family circumstances, and a chance to right the 'wrongs' of their own childhood. In addition, many additional, unexpected benefits such as closer family relations, and increased confidence and self-esteem were reported. By choosing a lifecourse within their own control, most reflected that their lives had changed immensely for the better. This would clearly support the argument posted by Ermisch and Pevalin (2003), in Chapter 1, that poverty and disadvantage *rather* than teenage pregnancy is responsible for some of the negative outcomes reported.

Based on these experiences, is it justifiable to try and discourage young people from becoming parents in such a situation? In cases where people are 'biologically' too young the argument can be made, for example, among people in their early teens where the health of the child and parent could be compromised. Indeed, it should be remembered that 'teenage' encompasses many years, and there could be different motivations and outcomes for a pregnant 13-year-old compared with a pregnant 19-year-old. However, most of the people in this study are of an age where pregnancy-related complications and health concerns are often less than those experienced by older parents (positive and uncomplicated pregnancy and birth

experiences were remarkably consistent throughout this research).

Taking a positive stance towards pregnancy in the teenage years, even if planned, would undoubtedly be controversial. It clearly challenges the rather negative, stereotypical view of teenage pregnancies and parenthood. A recent newspaper article summarises this challenging viewpoint. The references to poverty, job opportunities and education are particularly pertinent, and concur with the experiences of young people in this study. However, it should be added that educational aspiration can only be meaningful when there are attainable and realistic opportunities.

So when a girl at 17 decides to go ahead and have a baby, there is no tragedy of lost opportunity other than the local checkout till waiting for her low-paid labour. Why is it that in Labour's crusade against teenage pregnancy, it can't recognise that some of these teen mums are making reasonable – even moral – decisions about what they value in life, and what they want to do with their lives? How did opting for baby and motherhood over shelf-stacking ever become a tragedy? So, let's just call a spade a spade. The government may have good reasons for wanting to reduce teenage pregnancy, but they are not to do with lost opportunities. They are more likely to do with the extra cost to the state of the support required to ensure these vulnerable young mothers can do a good job of parenting their children. The government might, quite rightly, want to tackle entrenched inter-generational cycles of poverty, but the key to that is educational aspiration; teenage pregnancy is only a consequence of its absence. (Madeleine Bunting, *The Guardian*, 27 May 2005).

It is clear that young parents are stereotyped, and teenage pregnancy carries a stigma in society. However, it is also apparent that there are different views of this issue within different faiths and cultures in England. For example, in some cultures having children young within marriage does not carry a stigma. Interestingly,

Q5) *Before* you became pregnant, did you do anything to improve your health *in preparation for pregnancy?*

(Please tick *all* that apply):

❐ took folic acid

❐ stopped or cut down smoking

❐ stopped or cut down drinking alcohol

❐ ate more healthily

❐ sought medical/health advice

❐ took some other action, please describe _____

or

❐ I did not do any of the above *before* my pregnancy

In the next question, we ask about your partner – this might be (or have been) your husband, a partner you live with, a boyfriend, or someone you've had sex with once or twice.

Q6) *Before* I became pregnant …

(Please tick the statement which *most* applies to you):

❐ My partner and I had agreed that we would like me to be pregnant

❐ My partner and I had discussed having children together, but hadn't agreed for me to get pregnant

❐ We never discussed having children together

Q7) Please write your postcode (this will *not* be used to identify you)

Please write:

Q8) How old are you?

Would you like to help us with our research?

We are looking for young mums to take part in an interview about being a mum, your experiences and your support needs. The interviews will be very informal, completely confidential, will last roughly 30 minutes, and will be with a female interviewer.

If you are interviewed, you will receive a *£10 voucher* as a 'thank you'.

Please note that we will not be able to interview all those who volunteer.

....

Please write your details below if you would like to take part in an interview:

Name:

Age now:

Age at pregnancy:

Mobile telephone number:

Home telephone number (best time to ring):

(YOU DON'T HAVE TO FILL IN ALL OF THE ABOVE DETAILS, JUST THE ONE YOU WOULD PREFER US TO CONTACT YOU ON.)

Appendix B: Young father's questionnaire

Circumstances of partner's pregnancy

TSA is a research organisation based in Brighton. We are about to start some research into the support needs of young mothers and fathers. We would be grateful if you could help by completing this short questionnaire. TSA won't tell anyone your answers – it's completely confidential.

Below are some questions that ask about your circumstances and feelings around the time your partner became pregnant. This might be (or have been) your wife, a partner you live with, a girlfriend, or someone you've had sex with once or twice. **Please think of the current (or most recent) pregnancy when answering the questions below.**

Q1) In the month that your partner became pregnant ...
(Please tick the statement which *most* applies to you):
❑ I/we were not using contraception
❑ I/we were using contraception, but not on every occasion
❑ I/we always used contraception, but knew that the method had failed (that is, broke, moved, came off, came out, not worked etc) at least once
❑ I/we always used contraception

Q2) In terms of becoming a father, I feel that the pregnancy happened at the ...
(Please tick the statement which *most* applies to you):
❑ right time
❑ ok, but not quite right time
❑ wrong time

Q3) In terms of becoming a mother, did your partner feel that the pregnancy happened at the ...
(Please tick the statement which *most* applies to your partner):
❑ right time
❑ ok, but not quite right time
❑ wrong time

Q4) Just *before* your partner became pregnant ...
(Please tick the statement which *most* applies to you):
❑ I intended my partner to get pregnant
❑ my intentions kept changing
❑ I did not intend for my partner to get pregnant

Q5) Just before your partner became pregnant ...
(Please tick the statement which *most* applies to you):
❑ I wanted to have a baby
❑ I had mixed feelings about having a baby
❑ I did not want to have a baby